Soviet and Cuban Involvement in Africa

SOVIET MILITARY TRANSFERS 1980-85   ✖ SOVIET TREATIES OF FRIENDSHIP

◊ $5 BILLION - $10 BILLION   ▩ SOVIET MILITARY PERSONNEL

⬭ $1 BILLION - $5 BILLION   ▲ CUBAN MILITARY PERSONNEL

▯ $100 MILLION - $1 BILLION

Red Star Over Southern Africa

Red Star Over Southern Africa

by

Morgan Norval

Selous Foundation Press
Washington, D.C.

Typesetting by REF Typesetting & Publishing, Inc.
9400 Fairview Avenue, Manassas, VA 22110.

Cover design, maps and illustrations by William R. Wright.

Photos by Morgan Norval, Tom Schaaf, Jr., and Paratus.

Library of Congress Catalog Card Number: 87-51366.
ISBN: 0-944273-00-9.

This book was made possible by the generosity of the Selous Foundation, Kirby Foundation and the following individuals: James H. Beal, Page Bowie Clagett, Alice Carr Dyrsmid, Robert Fyke, Robert W. Galvin, Charles F. de Ganahl, Mrs. Ellen C. Garwood, F.M. Kirby, Robert H. Krieble, John Park, Jr., Fitzhugh Powell, Henry Salvatori, Elizabeth Smith and Ruth C. von Platen.

Books by Morgan Norval

Take My Gun If You Dare
Breaking the Stranglehold: The Liberation of Grenada
The Militia in 20th Century America

Books by Selous Foundation Press

Pinstripes and Reds:
An American Ambassador Caught Between the State
Department and the Romanian Communists, 1981-1985
by David B. Funderburk

To: **UNITA and RENAMO**—who are fighting for their freedom and independence from Soviet-sponsored Marxist tyranny and, by their example, are, hopefully, giving the West the courage to oppose the Soviet Union's worldwide imperialism.

Acknowledgements:

Thanks for their contributions and insights that went into this work go to many both here and in Africa. Among those are: Brian Adams, Klaus Crohn, Jeff Hill, Ollie Holmes, Ken Snowball, Tom Ferreira, Derick Elys, Willie Welgemoed, Johann Kruger, Tito Chingunji, Miguel N'Zau Puna, Figueiredo Paulo and Tom Schaaf, Jr.

I owe a special debt of gratitude to Dick Stephen and Nick Vorster for their valuable help on the peculiarities and importance of naval matters off the southern coast of Africa.

Finally, to Bob McKenna, friend and authority on special operations in southern Africa, a special note of thanks and a prediction: " Bob, one of these days in the near future we're finally going to win one."

The on-going struggle in southern Africa is against the brutal reality of Marxism and for Western values of democracy, freedom of speech, religion, the right to own one's own patch of ground and to enjoy the fruits of his labor. This book is about that battle.

Contents

Prologue

"The Communist ideology," Nobel laureate Aleksandr Solzhenitsyn reminds us, "is to destroy your society. This has been their aim for 125 years and has never changed; only the methods have changed a little. And what is ideological war? It is a focus of hatred, this is continued repetition of the oath to destroy the Western world."

This ideology, Solzhenitsyn says, is nothing more than ". . . a concentration of world evil, of hatred for humanity is taking place and it is fully determined to destroy your society . . . ."

Yet the appeasers of the Free World ignore the evil that Solzhenitsyn so vividly characterizes. Peace is possible with this empire, the appeasers insist. But how can you talk peace with an empire that is so beyond the pale of humanity that it is willing to manufacture mines in the shape of children's toys which they use to kill and maim children in Afghanistan. Are southern Africa's children to become the next victims of this monstrous policy? It is not beyond Gorbachev and the other grim men in the Kremlin to order the use of these hideous toys in Africa. It is the Marxist-Leninist socialist dogma that permits such atrocities and is the fuel that powers the Soviet onslaught toward the conquest of southern Africa.

This callous contempt for the children of the world illustrates the point too well that socialism's history is one of blood and violence. It is without question the most bloody, appalling movement in the history of mankind. This is the nightmare the Soviet Union is trying to impose upon the world! This nightmare is driven by the god-like ideology of Marxist-Leninist socialism. It is a godless pagan ideology; one that is drenched with blood and reeks of death and destruction.

Igor Shafarevich summed up the evil nature of socialism in his book *The Socialist Phenomenon,* unquestionably the most perceptive and significant work on the personal and cultural meaning of socialism ever written. He said, "The death of mankind is not only a conceivable result of the triumph of socialism—it constitutes the goal of socialism."

It is the evil force of Soviet Marxist-Leninist socialism that is assaulting southern Africa. This book will examine that evil at work in this area of vital concern to the free world.

Introduction

On April 9, 1241, the nimble horsemen of Prince Batu—grandson of Genghis Khan—and Mongol General Subadi attacked the combined forces of Poles and Germans at Wahlstat, near Liegnitz, Silesia. By dusk, the Poles and Germans were in full flight westward to Austria; their commander, Duke Henry II of Silesia, lay dead on the battlefield. The Mongols, masters of mobile, winter warfare, stood triumphantly.

Two days later, another Mongol force surprised and crushed King Bela IV of Hungary on the plain of Mohi—the road to Europe was open. Behind, to the east, lay death and destruction: Breslau was battered; Cracow, devastated; Kiev, gutted. The Principalities of Muroum, Yaroslaul, Muscovy and Kazan were ravaged.

The rest of Europe fearfully awaited the Mongol push westward toward the sea. Fortunately, after a summer interlude on the rich grasslands of Hungary, the Mongols swept eastward to the Lower Volga, subjugating Slovenia, Croatia and Bulgaria en route. Their advance through Eastern Europe halted only when news on the Great Khan's death reached the nomadic armies. To attend the quriltai, the council to elect his successor, the Mongol leaders turned back toward Russia. Providence, not fortitude, had spared the rest of Europe. Subsequent parcelling of the empire among Khan's descendants prevented them from ever returning.

****

The study of history helps us understand the present and predict the future. Russian history provides an explanation for current Soviet policy and events that are likely to transpire.

In 1238 A.D., medieval Russia was invaded and conquered by Mongol armies of the "Golden Horde" which held Moscow in thrall for more than two centuries. Russia was an intimate part of Christian Europe until it was separated by occupation armies of the conquering Mongols. The following 250 years of Mongol rule prevented influences from Europe, where relatively progressive political ideas were germinating, from contaminating traditional Russian life. The imprint of Mongol hooves was forever stamped on the soul of Mother Russia; while the Chinese, Indians, Persians, and Arabs eventually absorbed their Mongol conquerers, the Russians were Mongolized.

But Mongol subjugation taught the Russians enough to adopt their method and use it to overcome them when the Mongol empire became racked with bitter infighting among its rulers. To this day, the Russians remember the lessons of their teachers. Modern-day Soviet practices mirror the imperial methods of their Mongol ancestors—only the uniforms and technology have changed. Thus, Soviet activity can be predicted: Rule by terror, tribute collection and choke point control, all features of Mongol strategy, are by now well-known tactics of the Soviet Union.

The Soviets have relied on terror not only to seize power, but to retain it. A cardinal rule of Marxist-Leninist philosophy is that the state must rule the masses with a mailed fist full of violence and terror. In *Modern Times: The World from the Twenties to the Eighties*, Paul Johnson tells us that Lenin liberally quoted Robespierre, whose tortured mind conceived the Reign of Terror during the French Revolution: "The attribute of popular government in revolution is at one and the same time virtue and terror; virtue without terror is fatal, terror without virtue is impotent. The terror is nothing but justice, prompt, severe, inflexible; it is thus an emanation of virtue."

But Lenin need not have looked to French history for inspiration. The Mongols had mastered terrorism as well.

The Mongols exterminated entire populations if they did not surrender unconditionally. They would destroy, rather than defeat, opposing armies. Conquered lands were ruthlessly pacified. They periodically swept through vassal states, killing, looting and burning for no other reason than to remind their subjected who was in charge. Thoroughly terrorized people were paralyzed into submission. Likewise, the Soviets have taken up the terrorist methods of their Mongol forefathers. To expand "Russian" lands, they have murdered more than 60 million poeple in surrounding territories since the Bolshevik Revolution. To remind the people who was in charge, Stalin purged. Right now, the KGB is maintaining the balance of internal terror.

Tribute collection and caravan choke point controls were Mongol methods. Today's choke points are not caravan routes, where Mongols would perch collecting tolls, but sea lanes the Soviets wish to control. Choke points exist where sea lanes concentrate shipping in a limited area like the Cape of Good Hope. They are significant because they are hubs or nodes for world sea trading patterns—the "caravan routes" of the 20th century.

Formidable only because of overwhelming military power, the Mongols lived by exacting tribute on conquered caravan and commercial routes leading from Asia to Europe. In addition, they placed administrative centers in strategically important territories. Similar methods of imperial control were inherited by the Soviets, the 20th-century Mongols. Since the curse of communist society is its inability to grow enough food, keep technological pace with the West or produce enough consumer goods, the Soviets must rely on a mighty war machine so they can, in Mongol fashion, collect tribute in the form of food, technology and industrial goods. They exert dominion over the Red Empire with direct military threat; many Soviet satellites or client states harbor huge Soviet military bases.

The Mongols and Soviets attained global influence not by economic means, but military power combined with a willingness to use it remorselessly.

Another interesting similarity between Soviet and Mongol tactics is their efficient use of spies. The Mongol intelligence network infiltrated most of Europe; its excellence was without parallel. Spies generally operated under the guise of merchants and traders. Medieval Venetians, for example, were quite willing to sacrifice the interests of Europe for commercial advantage over their great rivals, the Genoese. In return for Mongol help in ousting the Genoese trade centers in the Crimea, the Venetians acted as part of the Mongol espionage service.

The Soviet intelligence network, the KGB, operates much the same way. Many multi-national corporations, such as the Ford Motor Company in National Socialist Germany and Bolshevik Russia, were and are willing to act like the Venetians so they can obtain monopolistic trade advantages over competitors and access to cheap labor in return for technology and military information.

In short, the Soviets' blueprint for the Marxist-Leninist global imperial drive are Genghis Khan's rules of war: an all-out assault on humanity. A "peaceful" world under Pax Sovietica would be nothing more than a tyrannical, tribute-collecting Pax Mongolica.

****

The ultimate objective of the Soviet Union is to establish a global, Marxist-Leninist dictatorship. It intends to accomplish this by indirect confrontation with the United States vis-a-vis subversion of Third World governments sitting astride vital choke points or those possessing strategic resources. Day by day, Soviets efforts to control strategic air and ocean choke points are increasingly more obvious.

Southern Africa, the focus of this book, has numerous natural resources and boasts one the world's most important choke points—the Cape of Good Hope. Between them, the Soviet Union and South Africa control more than 90 percent of the world's strategic resources. In addition, a significant amount of oil destined for the West is shipped through sea lanes around the Cape.

Using Mongol tactics of terror, tribute collection and choke point control, the Soviets have mounted a massive assault on this area of essential importance to the Free World. If successful, the Soviets could halt (and monopolize) the flow of strategic resources and oil to the West—events that would seriously disable the Western defense establishment. Reincarnated as the Soviets, the Mongols are on the move again, resembling the Golden Hordes of bygone days.

I hope this book will assist in the vast monumental task ahead—ensuring that the modern Mongols don't extinguish the flame of freedom.

Contact—a firefight with Marxist-Leninist terrorists in southern Africa.

Communist SWAPO terrorist killed by security forces in SWA/Namibia.

The security forces provide medical facilities and schools for the people in Ovamboland, SWA/Namibia.

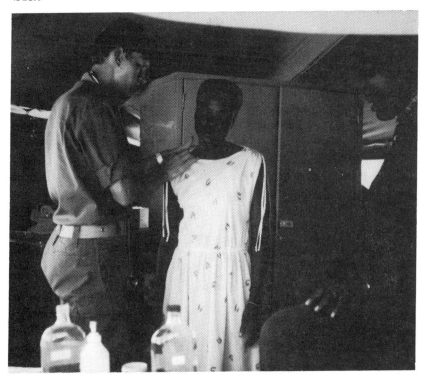

Soviet soldier in Angola

A group of SWAPO cadres sight-seeing in Moscow

1

Global Aims Of The Soviets

To understand Southern Africa's geopolitical importance to the Soviet Union, it is necessary to have a basic knowledge of Soviet global aims. The Soviet Union has never made secret its aim of world domination. It is fundamental Marxist doctrine that true peace cannot exist between Marxist and capitalist states. But Soviet neo-imperialism doesn't require direct confrontation to achieve its objectives. Like their spiritual ancestors, the Golden Horde, the Soviets are masters of the indirect strategy which, unfortunately, is so little understood by the West. For example, detente to the West is an end; to the Soviets detente is a means. Ceasefire to the West means the first step toward peace; ceasefire to the Soviets means the direct mode is unproductive and that a new manuever is required in the continuing struggle.

Circumstances permitting, the Soviets will exploit any crisis situation anywhere. They base their involvement on the degree of resistance they are likely to encounter from the West, and more specifically, the United States. Their game plan revolves mainly around their perception of the will of the U.S. to get involved. Since the end of World War II, Soviet strategy has been to attack, by indirect means, the backbone of the Free World—the United States.

This is best illustrated by the Soviets' action in Africa. There, using Cuban proxy armies, the Soviets have installed numerous communist dictatorships. In Angola, for example, Cubans installed the MPLA regime in 1975, and they remain, 35,000 strong, to this very day.

The establishment of Marxist-Leninist states, underwritten by surrogates whenever possible, is the first move of a global chess game which has no time limit and, unfortunately, is dominated by the Soviets due to a lack of Western will to effectively strike back.

Soviet strategy is to deny the U.S. freedom of action to respond to Soviet-supported imperialism throughout the world. This strategy is part and parcel of their ongoing conduct of World War III, which is not a war of massed armies, but instead, a series of terrorist acts and guerrilla-type insurgencies, or as the Soviets term them, "wars of national liberation."

World War III, from the Soviet point of view, encompasses three overlapping phases: containment, detente and double envelopment. Each cycle, or phase, lasted about twenty years. The first cycle, containment, commenced in 1946 and ended with the collapse of South Vietnam in 1975. The second stage, detente, as Henry Kissinger and the western world called it, dawned in 1960 when a U.S. Presidential Review Memorandum appeared advocating accommodation with the Soviet Union. This new policy, which replaced the policy of containment, was aimed at preserving the global status quo and fostering interdependence by expanding trade relations with Russia. U.S. efforts to reduce international tensions by accommodating the Soviet Union were accompanied by unilateral U.S. disarmament and appeasement of aggression. This policy has been followed by every American administration since Lyndon Johnson's.

The Cuban Missile Crisis of 1962 taught the Russians a hard lesson. Forced to retreat by overwhelming U.S. nuclear power, they resolved that such a reversal would be their last. They pursued a policy of military buildup and exported subversion abroad.

Between 1964 and 1979, under the guise of detente, the West retreated all over the globe. This retreat led to the collapse of the pro-Western, hard-line, anti-communist coalition: Indo-China, Angola, Mozambique, Guinea-Bissau, Rhodesia, Ethiopia, Aden, Afghanistan, Iran, Nicaragua, Grenada, Guyana and Surinam either fell directly to Marxist regimes or became implacable foes of the United States. In addition, the U.S. abandoned or alienated South Korea, Taiwan, South Africa, Brazil, Argentina and Chile during this time.

Detente finally collapsed when the Soviets invaded Afghanistan in 1979. But while the West sought a stalemate through detente, the Soviets, aided by a media campaign for peaceful co-existence eagerly trumpeted by the liberal Western media, plotted their next move.

As a result of the widening Sino-Soviet rift, the Soviets initiated the geographical encirclement of mainland China, the third phase of World War III, double envelopment. In this endeavor, they are aided by their new vassal states of Vietnam, Cambodia and Laos. During this period they accelerated nuclear and naval armaments programs. While the West dozed through the period of detente, the Soviets were busy working to catch up and surpass the West in military strength. SALT I recognized American-Soviet nuclear parity. SALT II codified military Soviet nuclear superiority. The Soviets' goal is absolute nuclear superiority. Their already comfortable second strike capacity of 1980 was expanded to third strike capability in 1982. Their game plan is clear: play a conventional nineteenth-century colonial ground game under the protective cover of an overwhelming 20th-century atomic umbrella.

As early as 1973, Leonid Brezhnev announced at a Communist conference in Prague that the USSR would achieve economic, military, and political hegemony by 1985 because the third and final stage of World War III, double envelopment (surround the Peoples Republic of China and strangle the West by severing the oil and ore supplies), was well advanced and would be complete by then. Brezhnev's timetable is off the mark, but the Soviets are moving toward their goal, as is evident by their successful colonization of Southern Africa and successful satellization of Nicaragua in our backyard.

Soviet actions during the containment phase fit the geopolitical theories of Sir Halford Mackinder, a turn-of-the-century geopolitical thinker. His theory posits the inner reaches of Eur-Asia (the Soviet Union) as the Heartland of a World Island.

Containment called for a series of interlocking alliances around the Rimland oceanic edge of the Eur-Asian continent that would isolate or check expansion from the Heartland, i.e., the Soviet Union. Composed of people dependent upon sea-borne transportation for their survival, the Rimland, or encircling allies—SEATO (South East Asia Treaty Organization), ANZUS (Australia, New Zealand and the United States), and the partners of the Rio de Janiero Treaty—would not only cooperate in containing the Heartland/Soviet Union, but strive to stabilize the globe by pursuing policies dedicated to free trade, private enterprise and democratic procedure. The Mackinder thesis projected a world in which sea power (America and its allies) and land power (the Soviet Union and its satellites) were in continuous conflict.

In 1946, the advantage lay with the West, for Mackinder's Heartland was open to air and nuclear attack and Anglo-American navies ruled the waves. They could counter any communist aggression along the Pacific and Indian Oceans or Atlantic shore of Eur-Asia. This state of affairs did not last long. By trying to accommodate the Soviet Union, U.S. nuclear and naval superiority slipped away. The alliance of advanced industrial states was confronted with a classical pre-missile, pre-atomic strategic situation in which the USSR could employ its more advantageous geographical location and its extensive, resource-laden land mass and large population against the West. The West stubbornly maintained that technology could overcome historical, geographic and strategic fundamentals.

According to Mackinder's thesis, whoever controlled the interior of Eur-Asia would eventually dominate the globe. He reasoned that the vast resources and interior lines of communications and supply would eventually permit the people who populated, organized, exploited and industrialized this area to strike out around the Rimland, gain access to the oceans and, by launching a blue water navy, overwhelm the surrounding sea people.

Mackinder's thesis was based upon an historical analysis of the success of nomadic steppe people from Central Asia who ravaged the rim of Eur-Asia for centuries. Attilla, Genghis Khan, Batu, Ulagu, Timar the Limper and Babar led their horsemen around the oceanic edge of Eur-Asia from the China Sea to the Indian Ocean and onto the Mediterranean and Adriatic. Stressing mobility and military might, these people disdained static agricultural pursuits. Instead, these tribes collected tribute from the people they had conquered. Occasionally these tribute-collecting tribes came together in a compact mass under the disciplined, central command of a dynamic leader. Then they exploded with brief, massive bursts of energy, sending them surging out of Central Asia to savage the surrounding civilizations.

These tribes, referred to by historians as Mongols, used tactics that swept almost all before their onrushing hordes. Feigned rout and flanking movements were standard maneuvers; cunning, intrigue and treachery were standard operating procedures. Mobility and an ability to deal with one foe at a time by radiating from Central Asia before opponents could combine were common tactics. The Mongols also employed trade missions and diplomatic envoys as spies and propagandists. These fifth columnists often prepared the path of conquest through the clever use of psychological warfare, a typical Mongol technique.

****

Masters of mobility and deceit, these nomadic Mongols conquered and controlled the caravan routes and commercial crossroads that connected the advanced societies on the coasts of the continent. They lived by levying tribute, not by peaceful productivity.

The modern Soviet-Mongols also live by conquest, not by peaceful productivity. The reason for this is the nature of the economic system the modern Mongols have imposed upon themselves. That system is the totalitarian one of Marxist-Leninist socialism which requires expansion, conquest, and parasitism for its survival.

Socialism, which finds its most faithful expression in the Soviet Union, depends upon parasitism. The socialist state survives for a time either by being a parasite on its people to the point of their economic destruction, or by being a parasite on some rich state which continues to bail them out, as the United States has done continually since the end of the Second World War.

This parasitism has a dark, ugly side in that it leads to

imperialism: the parasite socialist state, as the Soviet Union amply demonstrates, needs new, healthy bodies to feed upon. As it destroys one, it moves on to destroy another. The ultimate conclusion of the socialist order is death and destruction, a goal required by its very nature.

It is the aim of the Soviets to defeat, not destroy the West. Tribute collection, not atomic rubble is their aim. The Soviets seek to preserve the West's productive plant in order to feed and prop up their own economy.

The curse of communism is starvation and a slave-like existence. Nevertheless, aided by certain international financiers who have loaned the USSR some $60 billion since 1970 and abetted by many multinational corporations which have sold the Soviets advanced high-level technology, Soviet Russia is seizing control of the sea lanes and strategic areas of the globe upon which the developed nations depend.

They are using so-called wars of liberation, conducted by their Cuban mercenary stooges, to carry out their goals.

Choke point control and tribute collection are Mongol tactical methods which the Soviets are using in large measure with naval forces. Suddenly, the Soviets have emerged as a great naval power. Realizing the importance of sea power, they have applied Mongol tactics to the maritime world, using their naval mobility to effect choke point control of the Seven Seas. Only a short time ago, the Soviet Navy was, at best, a coastal defense force.

While the United States was reducing its naval forces prior to the election of Ronald Reagan, the Soviets embarked upon a massive naval expansion program that produced spectacular results. The Soviet Pacific fleet is larger than the United States Navy—indeed, Soviet naval forces outnumber the U.S. in virtually every category except aircraft carriers.

The same trend is reflected in the strength of the respective maritime fleets. In 1950, the U.S. had 3,500 commercial ships to the Soviets' 400. In 1984, the Soviets had 2,500 to our 572, a number that has declined since then. In addition, the Soviet merchant fleet is modern and able to be quickly converted into military transports, in contrast to the aging and outdated U.S. merchant fleet.

The Soviet fishing fleet is larger and more active than the

fishing fleets of all other nations combined.

In the past, the Soviet Union, as a self-contained energy- and mineral-independent land power, needed nothing more. Now Soviet task forces cruise sea lanes of communication in the Pacific, Indian and Atlantic Oceans—sea lanes that carry the oil and ore vital to the very existence of America and its allies. Even America is vulnerable, for the U.S. imports 40 percent of its petroleum and many of its strategic minerals.

(The tremendous increase in the size of the Soviet merchant fleet could permit its use in a possible new strategy of choke-point control. It is a subtle and simple strategy: if most merchant ships carrying goods on certain trade routes are Soviet-controlled, that route is effectively "choked." While the numbers in Western fleets decline, the Soviets are expanding, capturing more of the shipping trade and undercutting the prices charged by their Free World competition. The strategy doesn't sound farfetched.)

Most seaborne commerce flows through fifteen funnels or choke points. Five inland seas (South China, Mediterranean, North, Norwegian and Caribbean), eight critical passage points (Malacca Straights, Ceylon, Horn of Africa, Mozambique Channel, Cape of Good Hope, Gibraltar, Cape Horn and Straights of Florida) along with two inter-oceanic canals (Suez and Panama) dominate the world's maritime traffic. These sea lanes link the industrialized states of the Western Pacific, Western Europe and the Western Hemisphere. Since 1964, the Soviets have moved quietly to expand their influence in all fifteen of these vital choke points. They have moved to the sea with one goal: total isolation of the United States.

Sea choke points are the keys to the geopolitical future of the West. Cutting off the traffic in food, the "irreducible essential," might not prove fatal to the agriculturally self-sufficient. But interdicting the flow of raw material would have an effect of global proportions—the essential industries in the West would erode and crumble.

A strategy to deal with this reality does not have to concern itself unduly with peaceful augmentation of national assets and national power. Rather, a realistic strategy based on the recognition of the importance of the sea and other choke points can and should deal with the possibility of coercive methods, including Finlandization.

One must not overlook the final two dimensions with which strategy, both the Soviets' and our own, has to concern itself. These are the air and space blankets that enshroud the earth.

DeSeversky, an early pioneer of aviation, correctly predicted the importance of air blankets as man mastered flight. At the same time, DeSeversky, a child of the air age, failed to measure the role of space travel and sophisticated technology such as satellites in the modern economy and geostrategic balance. By implication, DeSeversky projected the view that the United States would be going it alone in a future conflict. Alliances did not weigh heavily on the scales with which he calculated the possible alternatives. Four decades after *Air Power: Key to Survival* (*Victory Through Air Power,* Maj. Alexander P. DeSeversky, Simon & Schuster, New York, 1942) appeared in print, his strategy must be revised to include a more realistic fact. The United States cannot "go it alone" in either peace or war. There exists a vast network of ties, including those requiring the use of air lanes, linking the United States to dozens of other countries in commercial, geopolitical, cultural and other ways. In case of war, the network would eventually bind the United States and its political and spiritual allies in military ways.

For convenience one can speak of Aerial Skyways of Transport and Resupply (ASTAR). Because sea and air lanes empty into similar junction and transit points, Sea Lanes of Communication (SLOC) and ASTAR broadly correspond. Thus, the world's fifteen sea choke points have their counterparts in the air.

The Soviet Union recognizes the importance of air choke points. For example, they have stationed a Kiev-class Vertical Takeoff or Landing (VTOL) carrier in Cam Ranh Bay, Vietnam. In a matter of days, this ship could be sitting below vital airlanes in the Pacific. Other Kiev-class carriers could be deployed in the Atlantic and pose a threat to the customary northern commerical air path from New York to Europe and to "the alternative southern route from Miami, Atlanta, and New York north of the Azores and Morocco."

(A well-planned free-world counter-strategy must include recognition that the air dimension provides the road to space.)

The fall of Saigon to the communists in April 1975, followed by most of Indochina, ended the containment phase and nearly completed the geographical encirclement of the People's Republic of China. This endangered oil and ore supply routes through the South China Sea to Japan, from Iran, Arabia, South Africa and South America.

Mainland China, an ancient adversary of the Soviet Union, is surrounded by Soviet power. A sharp sickle of Russian bases, satellites and allies curves west, south, then east around mainland China from the Sea of Japan to the south China sea. They include Shikotan, Sakhalin, Sikote, Alin, North Korea, Mongolia, Siberia, Afghanistan, India and Soviet Indochina, beginning at the Tartar Strait and closing at Cam Ranh Bay. Only two holes remain in this hostile perimeter, both to the south. Pro-Chinese Pakistan, threatened by a Soviet-backed Baluchi uprising, and non-aligned Burma, also under communist guerrilla attack, provide Peking with uncertain avenues to the Indian Ocean and to the maritime nations of the Western Alliance.

Just south of Free China, or Taiwan, lies the South China Sea, which is dominated by Soviet carrier battle groups. To the north, from Taiwan to South Korea, lies the East China Sea—mainland China's only access route to western technology, food and goods. Without these items, the Balkanization of China can begin in short order. Ironically, Taiwanese control of the East China Sea would be the key to Red China's survival.

In Afghanistan, the Soviets are beginning to clear their southern flank for a push toward the Persian Gulf. The oil of the Middle East beckons. The warm waters of the Indian Ocean call. The strategy is sound. First, insure the eastern flank in Afghanistan; second, secure the western wing by seizing Yugoslavia, and then advance to the Adriatic which would destabilize Greece and neutralize Turkey; then drive on through Iran to the Indian Ocean.

Western Europe, heavily dependent on the Middle East for petroleum, hooked on natural gas from the Soviet Union, and confronted with Warsaw Pact forces poised to strike, will, for their own survival and self-interest, slip into the Soviets' satellite orbit.

This is not the end of the potential trouble for the West that would result from the Soviet-Mongol strategy. Most minerals essential to an industrialized society are located in Southern Africa near a vital choke point. Until 1965, facilities in Africa that monitored mineral shipments to the West were under the sovereignty of the sea peoples. In addition, oil from the Persian Gulf went mainly to Japan and Western Europe by way of the South China Sea, the Suez Canal and the Mediterranean. A minimal amount was exported to the United States.

Beginning in 1965, energy consumption and petroleum transport were revolutionized. Oil that had been moved through the Suez and Mediterranean to Western Europe came southward in supertankers along East Africa, through the Mozambique Channel, around the Cape of Good Hope and up the west coast of Africa, via the South Atlantic Ocean, past Angola and Guinea-Bissau, to NATO and the United States. Hostile ports-of-call replaced friendly naval facilities.

The Soviets have aggressively moved to the sea and are seeking to Finlandize the western industrialized nations via choke point control and seizing the strategic resources upon which the wheels of commerce of our society turn.

Eventually, the Soviets will establish world hegemony by indirectly confronting the U.S. through so-called wars of liberation in Third World nations sitting astride vital choke points or possessing needed resources.

A seminal work of communist theory, *The World Communist Movement: An Outline of Strategy and Tactics* by V.V. Zagladin, lucidly explains the role of national liberation movements in furthering the world goals of Soviet-Mongol imperialism. The language is so clear and specific that the continuing debate in the West over the question of Soviet manipulation of these movements can only be explained as a triumph of Soviet propaganda.

"The social revolution," Lenin stressed, "can come only in the form of an epoch in which are combined civil war by the proletariat against the bourgeoisie in the advanced countries and a whole series of democratic and revolutionary movements, including the national-liberation movements in the undeveloped, backward and oppressed nations."[1] Communism's role in the development of national liberation movements was stressed by Lenin. "Revolutionary movement of peoples of the East can now develop effectively, can reach a successful issue, only in direct association with the revolutionary struggle of our Soviet Republic against international imperialism."[2]

Today, Soviet theoreticians still toe the line drawn by Lenin more than six decades ago. Alexei Kozlov, writing in the Soviet weekly journal *New Times* , stressed the importance of Soviet control of revolutionary movements: "Solidarity with the liberation movements of the peoples of Asia, Africa, and Latin America is a permanent area of the collective action of the Communist parties. . . .

"The revolutionary democrats are guided in their activities by the doctrine of scientific socialism, by the organizational and political principles of the building of the alliance with world socialism and the international Communist movement."[3]

The American sovietologist Dr. Peter Vanneman told the U.S. Senate's Subcommittee on Security and Terrorism that "the USSR is striving to enhance its influence in southern Arica not merely to affect events there but to influence events throughout the continent and the world. Its purpose is not merely to dominate the southern African region, but to utilize its influence there to enhance its influence elsewhere.

"In other words, Soviet activities in the southern African region reflect that regime's concern with fashioning policies for areas far from its periphery which will maximize its global influence. As a global superpower, the USSR must devise policies for far-flung areas which will augment its influence in areas of its vital interests throughout the world. The problem is to exploit local conflict to expand global, continental and regional influence.

"The intensity of the continuing long range interest of the USSR in southern Africa," Dr. Vanneman told the subcommittee, "is indicated by the creation of three relatively new governmental structures organized specifically to deal with that area of the world. There is a special section of the African Institute of the USSR Academy of Science that deals with 'liberation questions,' and the largest section of INU, a department of the KGB dealing with propaganda, is the one for southern Africa. Finally, one of the three sections of the Soviet Foreign ministry dealing with Africa focuses exclusively on southern Africa."[4]

Southern Africa is a storehouse of strategic minerals. Many of the minerals—chrome, cobalt, ferro-manganese, nickel, vanadium and titanium—are duplicated in commercial quantities only in the Soviet Bloc. Thus, satellization of Southern Africa would enable the Soviet Union to establish a communist mineral cartel with which they could control the West. The Republic of South Africa, moreover, sits astride the supertanker sea routes from the Middle East. They run southward through the Indian Ocean along the East African coast, through the Mozambique Channel, and around the Cape of Good Hope before angling northward into the Atlantic Ocean. They travel past Namibia, Angola and Guinea-Bissau, terminating in the United States or Western Europe.

Thus, the independence of Southern Africa and the re-integration of South Africa into the Western alliance is essential to Western survival.

The Soviets have moved to isolate South Africa. Angola, Zimbabwe and Mozambique have fallen to Soviet-backed forces. If the Red tide surges over Southern Africa, the Soviets will have buried the treasure chest of the West. The modern day Mongols—the Soviets—would be in a position to collect tribute from a humble West, begging for essentials to keep its industrial base from collapsing.

1. V. Zaaladin, *The World Communist Movement: An Outline of Strategy and Tactics.* (Moscow, U.S.S.R.: Progress Publishers, 1973) pp. 74-75.

2. V.I. Lenin, *Collected Works*, Vol. 30, Progress Publishers, Moscow 1975, p. 151.

3. Alexei Kozlov, "With Confident Stride: The International Communist Movement Today," *New Times*, No. 20-1981.

4. *Soviet, East German and Cuban Involvement in Fomenting Terrorism*

in Southern Africa. Report of the Chairman of the Subcommittee on Security and Terrorism, U.S. Senate Judiciary Committee, 97th Congress, 2nd session (November 1982).

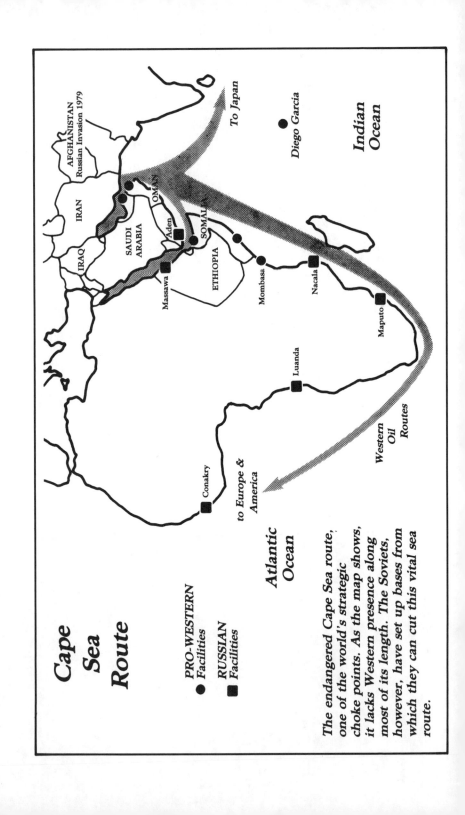

Cape Sea Route

PRO-WESTERN Facilities ●

RUSSIAN Facilities ■

The endangered Cape Sea route, one of the world's strategic choke points. As the map shows, it lacks Western presence along most of its length. The Soviets, however, have set up bases from which they can cut this vital sea route.

Indian Ocean

Atlantic Ocean

To Japan

Diego Garcia

AFGHANISTAN Russian Invasion 1979

IRAN

IRAQ

SAUDI ARABIA

OMAN

Aden

SOMALIA

ETHIOPIA

Massawa

Mombasa

Nacala

Maputo

Luanda

Conakry

to Europe & America

Western Oil Routes

Korean-War era Shackelton, a propeller-driven air-plane used for air-sea rescue operations off the south-ern tip of Africa. These planes were grounded in November 1984 as they were falling apart. Because of the UN Arms Embargo, South Africa can't purchase any long-distance patrol planes, and now there are no longer any air-sea rescue planes available to service ships in trouble in the treacherous waters of the vital Cape Sea route.

Soviet Bloc fishing ships lying off the harbour of Walvis Bay. Soviet Bloc fishing ships are over-fishing the waters off the coast of Angola and South West Africa/Namibia, destroying the local fishing industry in those countries.

2
Choke Point Control: Cutting the Cape Sea Route

The gifts of geography and geology have combined to give the Republic of South Africa an enormous impact on the destiny of the West. It not only sits astride the vital Cape of Good Hope sea route off the southern tip of Africa, but is the important source of many non-fuel minerals vital to industry and national security.

The West, especially our European NATO allies, depend upon the following goods that travel the Cape sea route:

- 60 percent of their total oil consumption
- 70 percent of their strategic minerals
- 25 percent of their food supplies.

Twenty percent of American oil requirements pass via the Cape route within 20 miles of Cape Town. More than 12,000 ships per year pass around Cape Point, making it one of the busiest sea routes in world commerce. Sea-going vessels rely on facilities in the Republic of South Africa for fuel, supplies, weather reports and rescue services almost non-existent elsewhere.

Already, fully 60 percent of the oil destined for the West is shipped around the Cape of Good Hope. Huge supertankers and large-bulk container ships can't pass through the Suez Canal, however, and must make the longer trip around the Cape to either Europe or the Americas. Many analysts today believe that in the event of a conflict in the Middle East that closes the Suez Canal, the rest of the oil from the Middle East would travel around the Cape sea route. Of course, as long as the Suez Canal is open, shippers will obviously choose that route over the longer one around the Cape.

There is little doubt that the Suez Canal is already in jeopardy. Soviet-controlled Ethiopia is dangerously close to the Suez Canal. Availability to the Soviets of the Ethiopian naval base at Massawa extends their reach from the Red Sea to the southern end of the Canal. The USSR has also taken over the former British base in Aden when the British withdrew their forces from "east of the Suez." Moscow quickly stepped into the power vacuum caused by the British withdrawal and is pre-positioned to cut off Middle East oil shipments at their source. In short, the Soviets can close the Suez Canal if they so desire.

Thus it could be argued that the Soviets' strategic presence in the Middle East has already enabled them to cut off the oil routes to the West. Under this scenario, some would say, the United States has no vital interests in the southern tip of Africa.

Southern Africa, or more specifically, the Republic of South Africa, supplies essential ingredients to build modern technological goods. Home computers, refrigerators and automobiles could not be built without essential minerals supplied by South Africa.

At the present time, the United States is in the unenviable position of being increasingly dependent on foreign countries, including the Republic of South Africa, more for certain non-fuel substances, called strategic minerals, than for oil. This fact is of concern to the U.S. Congress, as evidenced by the House Committee on Mines and Minerals' 1980 report "Sub-Saharan Africa: Its role in Critical Mineral Needs of the Western World."

It said: "No issue facing America in the decades ahead poses the risks and dangers to the national economy and defense presented by this nation's dependence on foreign sources for strategic and critical minerals. America is now dependent on foreign sources in excess of 50 percent of 24 of the 32 minerals essential to national survival. Minerals such as manganese—essential in the production of steel (import dependence 98 percent); cobalt—vital hardener and strengthener of steels (import dependence 95 percent); and chromium—indispensable to the production of stainless steel and the least substitutable of all ferro-alloys (import dependence 90 percent) reveal a vulnerability more serious than the energy crisis.

"While America may develop its own alternative energy resources," the report concluded, "in many cases there are no substitutes for the minerals imported from foreign sources, countries which are often unstable at best and hostile at worst."

Significantly, many of these strategic minerals are found in the Soviet Union, one of its colonies, or in the southern Africa region, especially the Republic of South Africa.

South Africa is a treasure house of minerals vital to the prosperity and very existence of the Western industrial nations. Its critical role as a reliable source of minerals is portrayed in Table 1, showing the percentage of the world's mineral reserve and production that would be held by Soviet South Africa.

Table 1
Hypothetical Soviet Control Over Mineral Production
and Reserves Shown as Percentage of World Figures
(If USSR acquired control of South Africa)

MINERAL	PRODUCTION %	RESERVES %
Platinum	94	99
Chrome	67	84
Manganese	62	93
Gold	72	68
Vanadium	70	97
Fluorspar	26	50
Iron Ore	35	46
Asbestos	47	35
Uranium	43	17

Since South Africa's minerals are vital to the West's industrial base, it should be obvious that for these minerals to be of any use to the United States, they must get from South Africa to their final destination for processing and utilization. For this, we need the Cape sea route.

The minerals leave South Africa from two major ports: Richards Bay, on the Indian Ocean, and Saldanha Bay, on the Atlantic Ocean. Minerals leaving these and other South African ports must travel all or part of the Cape sea route.

Whose responsibility is it to protect this vital route? In 1957 when the British gave its Simons Town naval base to the South Africans, the Earl of Selkirk, then First Lord of the Admiralty, said, "The defence of the vital sea route around the Cape can be assured only if the task and responsibilities which it entails are shared. That is what we are doing here and that is what we believe will be achieved." It was anticipated that the Royal Navy would continue using Simons Town and, together with the South African Navy, would share the responsibility of protecting this vital sea route.

British participation came to a halt in 1975 when Harold Wilson's socialist government pulled out. For good measure, the Royal Navy joined the U.S. Navy, and stopped visiting South African ports.

After the pullout, the South African Navy lost all contact with its NATO counterparts and no longer participated in joint training exercises. The inevitable result was a steady erosion of the combat readiness of the South African Navy.

Let those who are so quick to condemn us, they reasoned, assume the protection of the Cape sea route. The South African Navy has literally turned its back on its former blue water role and voluntarily scaled itself down to a coastal defense role.

South African officials saw no reason for protecting the Cape sea route and southern Indian and Atlantic oceans. What was the point of trying to keep an alternative to Suez open for countries so ready to punish and excoriate the freest country in Southern Africa?

The Republic of South Africa decided to redesign its naval strategy and build a new navy designed to support South African regional interests. Because of the 1977 United Nations Arms Embargo, no spare parts would be forthcoming for the British and French-type ships in the South African Navy. So, a major shipbuilding program was set into motion. Ships were repaired using locally produced components, in many cases at a fraction of the cost of imported items. The result was, and is, a steady supply of new ships coming into commission specifically designed to meet and match any threat arising from Soviet-oriented colonies to the north.

By renouncing its shared responsibilities of protecting the Cape sea lanes, South Africa has dumped a full-sized stratigic problem in the lap of the sanctimonious West.

There is yet another fact that should be included in Western strategic thinking. Except for railways inside the Republic of South Africa, there is virtually no north-south inland transportation infrastructure in Africa. So sea routes along the coasts are absolutely critical to many nations, since the only way to move goods is to ship them. Control of these vital sea lanes by a hostile power could adversely affect many African allies of the West.

How is this vital sea route going to be protected? As the leader of the Western Alliance and one of South Africa's harshest critics, it would seem the United States would inherit that sticky chore. Even President Reagan said as much: "Freedom to use the seas is our nation's lifeblood. For that reason, our navy is designed to keep the sea lanes open worldwide; a far greater task than closing those sea lanes at strategic choke points, maritime superiority for us is a necessity."

Unfortunately, neither Reagan's rhetoric nor Congress's South Africa bashing can make the naval situation in this strategic area go away. Reality is much more frightening.

Thanks to the presence of two Soviet colonies, Angola and Mozambique, and the self-imposed U.S.-British naval boycott of South African ports, 5,000 miles of the Cape shipping route from Sierra Leone to Kenya is lacking a significant Western naval presence.

If the Suez Canal is closed again, or the Red Sea mined again, Western ships would have to run a gauntlet through Soviet-controlled areas such as the Mozambique Channel between Madagascar and Mozambique, or past Angola, Soa Tome, then Cuba in the West. Only the southern tip, the mineral treasure house of the West, will remain free as we know it. Soviet planners are well aware of this even as our own shortsighted, morally posturing politicians choose to ignore it.

While the United States was reducing the size of its fleet from 951 ships in 1968 to 496 in 1976, the Soviets embarked on a massive naval expansion. Now they boast a large, modern, blue-water fleet that "shows the flag" across the world's oceans.

The Russians have secured several naval facilities in the Middle East, on the Horn of Africa, on both coasts of Africa, and in the Indian Ocean, from which they threaten shipping in the southern Indian Ocean and, with bases in Maputo (Mozambique) and Luanda (Angola), pose a serious threat to the Cape shipping route.

Thanks to Russia's naval presence and Western political attitudes toward the Republic of South Africa, Western maritime forces, of which the U.S. Navy is the largest, find themselves with an ever-decreasing availability of secure base facilities.

Indian Ocean-going U.S. naval forces denied access to South African ports must rely on Diego Garcia and Australian facilities. Unfortunately, these facilities are a long way from oil fields in the Middle East and mineral deposits of southern Africa.

Diego Garcia also suffers from inherent shortcomings as a major operational naval base: 1) it is a small, completely isolated support facility with neither human nor industrial back-up infrastructure; 2) everything from spare parts to food must be imported; 3) supply lines to Diego Garcia are prohibitively long: They can be cut and the facility rendered ineffective.

But the presence of excellent port facilities in South Africa can render this nightmare a forgotten dream. The South African naval base at Simons Town can be the key to an effective free world presence in the Indian and south Atlantic Oceans. Simons Town offers the finest docking and maintenance facilities between Singapore and the Straights of Gibraltar.

Apart from Simons Town, there are six other large, highly-developed, deep-water harbors on the coastline of South Africa. The most noteworthy are Cape Town and

Durban, which have extensive facilities including drydocks for vessels too large for Simons Town.

Also important is the fact that these harbors have highly sophisticated industrial and commercial cities around them. This facilitates repair, maintenance and recreational requirements of a fleet and its personnel.

Given the deteriorating strategic situation in the Indian and south Atlantic Oceans, the U.S. and NATO should revise their naval policy vis-a-vis the Republic of South Africa. To do so would require a change of political attitude toward the government in Pretoria—a change requiring a politically courageous administration that would take the crucial and necessary steps to restore our presence in southern Africa.

Strategic deficiencies will not go away. And so long as U.S. foreign policy in southern Africa is determined by the radical left—the hate South Africa Crowd—the West will suffer.

Only when we in the West begin to determine our vital interests in an emotionless way can constructive action be taken to correct the strategic imbalance now favoring the Soviet Union.

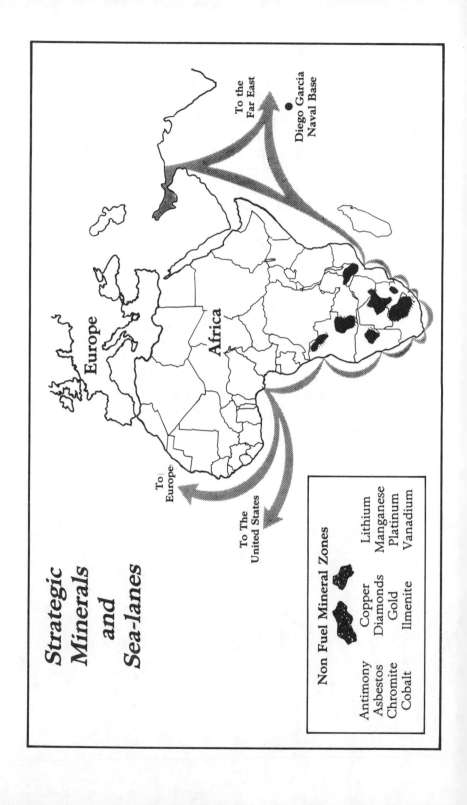

Strategic
Minerals
and
Sea-lanes

To the
Far East

Diego Garcia
Naval Base

Europe

Africa

To
Europe

To The
United States

Non Fuel Mineral Zones

Antimony   Copper   Lithium
Asbestos   Diamonds   Manganese
Chromite   Gold   Platinum
Cobalt   Ilmenite   Vanadium

When super tanker loaded with crude oil
gets caught on the crest of two waves.

The weight of the crude can cause
the ship to break in two.

Russian diesel-powered Foxtrot submarine; one of these could cut the Cape Sea Route.

Simons Town Naval Base, RSA

3
How One Sub Can Cut The Cape Sea Route

Nine years after Portuguese navigator-explorer Bartholomeu Dias passed what is now the Cape of Good Hope, Vasco da Gama, en route to India, landed at the Cape. Thus began the era of sea trade between the East and Europe.

During the 1500's, Portugal shipped an enormous amount of wealth from the Spice Island, India, Java and the East back to Europe. Thanks to the pluck of their sailors, Portugal became a major maritime nation because of this trade around the southern tip of Africa.

Other European nations soon took notice and decided to grab a share of the trade with the East Indies. In 1600, England chartered the East India Company. Two years later, the Dutch began trading along this route under the guise of the United East India Company. A stubborn, bloody fight ensued among the three countries for control of this lucrative trade.

Yet, one strange fact emerged from this intense struggle to dominate the sea trade with the East—none of them occupied the Cape of Good Hope. Nor did they attempt to arm it as a base to raid enemy commerce. This is an astounding fact to consider: Three maritime nations were at war with one another, rounding the Cape on their way to or from home, and none had established a base at this strategic spot! Considering the booty available to ships traveling the Cape, this oversight borders on the incredible.

Fully-laden ships traveled the Cape en route to Europe with almost no confrontation of any kind. In almost 200 years of intense commercial rivalry and bloody warfare both in

Asia and Europe, only one ship was sunk at the Cape by enemy action.

So this strategic spot, which dominated the trade routes and was also capable of succoring that commerce, lay neglected, waiting to be taken by any nation willing to claim it. But none did because none of the seafaring nations of the day could see the area as vital to their purposes!

During the American Civil War, the Captain of the Confederate naval raider C.S.S. *Alabama*, Raphael Semmes, realized the importance of the Cape area as a base from which to raid enemy commerce. He used Simons Town to refit and re-provision the *Alabama* before proceeding to India to interdict the Union's East India trade. In his diary, Semmes made it quite clear that his raiding foray to India would have been impossible without his utilization of the Simons Town facilities.

The miracle of the Cape in the 16th and 17th centuries was that no seafaring nation wanted it. The chilling thought in the late 20th-century is that a new seafaring nation, the Soviet Union, does.

Lacking actual physical possession of the Cape, the Soviets have the naval capability to cut the Cape sea route. In fact, they could cut it with just one submarine, a vessel they have in large numbers in their fleet.

Geography, climate and oceanography combine to create very treacherous seas off the Cape. This is due to the convergence of the warm Agulhas current from the Indian Ocean, flowing southward down the east coast of Africa, with the cold waters of the Benguela current moving up from the Antarctic into the Atlantic Ocean. Add to this mixture huge nasty swells caused by weather that originates in the south polar regions and conditions for extremely hazardous shipping are created at the southern tip of Africa.

What often happens is that strong winds blowing from the southwest will push the cold waters from the South Atlantic further to the east past the Cape of Good Hope, in some cases actually part of the way up the Indian Ocean coast of South Africa. This will cause considerable mixing with the warm waters flowing south from the Indian Ocean. This mixing effect is enhanced due to the narrowness of the continental shelf off the east coast of South Africa (roughly the area from Port Elizabeth along the coast past Durban). Not only is the continental shelf narrow, but it plunges steeply to the ocean depths of this region. It is thus narrow and steep. The movement and mixing of the waters along this steep continental slope with its resulting undersea turbulence enable a submarine to avoid detection. There it would lie waiting for ships right up against the shelf in close range of its targets—shipping leaving South African ports and the maritime ships sailing the busy sea lanes around the southern tip of Africa.

From these positions a Soviet submarine could seriously disrupt, if not close, the Cape sea route. The sub could sow delay-activated mines in the mouths of the South African ports and, using these mines and its torpedoes, subject South African ports to a naval blockade.

Nautical charts for the region, for example, recommend that oil tankers stay in shipping lanes that only extend ten miles from the coast. The reason for this is that wave crests caused by sea swells farther south are sometimes one half mile or more apart. If a huge supertanker, heavily laden with crude oil, gets caught in these types of swells, it can break in two.

Huge-bulk cargo container ships are also advised to stay close to shore as the tremendous swells and high winds farther off the coast can cause the containers to be blown off the ship.

The southern tip of Africa is about 350 miles from the "Roaring Forties"—that is, 40 degrees of latitude south. Stormy gale conditions exist here at least 60 percent of the time. That means gale-force winds at least 60 percent of the time. These winds create huge, high waves that can sink merchant ships, especially supertankers, and strip bulk cargo ships of their cargo containers. Even ordinary merchant ships are not immune from the danger caused by these terrible climatic conditions.

A ship can weather these waves by either sailing diagonally across them or by sailing into them head-on. Both ways can turn into disaster.

When a ship heads directly into the wave, its bow (front

part of the ship) often will disappear under the wave as a wall of water plunges over it. If the ship can't shed this water quickly—in a matter of seconds—it can have its bow sheared off by the weight of the water on its deck. (A cubic meter of water weighs more than one metric ton. Thus, a huge wave can almost instantaneously deposit a lot of weight on that submerged part of the ship.) Merchant ships are designed differently from warships. They are usually wider and have solid metal railing along their decking so the crew won't fall overboard. A warship had open spaces with chains strung from poles, instead of solid railing, along the sides of the ship. The result is that water quickly flows off the warship back into the sea. The solid railing of the merchant ship can hold the water for a critical period of time and, if the amount and thus the weight is sufficient it can, and on numerous occasions has, sheared the bow off unfortunate merchant ships.

If the ship is traveling diagonally across the wave, it must be steered with great skill. If it is not and the ship gets caught by waves smacking perpendicularly into its sides, it can flounder. This can be a deadly serious problem with the huge unwieldy supertankers with their cargo of heavy crude oil.

Huge waves smashing directly into the side of the ship cause it to tilt over in the direction the wave is traveling. Warships are so designed that they quickly return to their normal positions. Merchant ships return upright at a slower rate. If the ship is hit by another wave before it gets upright, it is driven further over on its side. If the waves are strong enough and frequent enough, they can flip the ship over.

The convergence of the cold Benguela and warm Agulhas currents, combined with narrow shipping lanes, creates fantastic conditions for submariners and enormous problems for those conducting anti-submarine warfare.

The mixing of waters is so thorough that in one instance, during anti-submarine exercises conducted by the South African Navy, one of its conventional-powered diesel subs came within 500 yards of the hunting frigate before it was positively identified. This is point-blank range for a hostile sub! It was not the fault of South African sonar operations; it is the hydrographic conditions created by the mixture of the cold and warm water. The temperature of the water affects sonar echoes. Under ideal conditions, the sonar echo will be of such a nature that underwater detection presents few problems.

However, waters of different temperatures that are mixed by swirling, converging currents create inversion layers, in which cold waters may lie atop warm water. In turn, the sonar echoes produced by such waters can become undecipherable. Anti-submarine detection under these circumstances can be impossible and the advantage swings drastically in favor of the lurking submarine.

A smart sub skipper will find one of these inversion layers, hide in it and use his passive sonar to locate his target. Since he is "running silently," he uses noise generated by the target ship as his guide. He will remain quiet until he launches his deadly torpedoes. If the hostile sub is diesel-powered, he has another advantage: they are much quieter than nuclear-powered subs. These factors all combine to make the waters off the southern tip of Africa an ideal area for submarine warfare, with the advantage overwhelmingly in favor of the submariner.

It is not uncommon for inversion layers to float within fifty feet of the surface of the sea. This is periscope depth for submarines, which means one could hide, undetected, at periscope depth, waiting for its prey. This danger is heightened when one realizes that not only does the South African Navy lack an anti-submarine capability, but it has been ten years or more since any joint naval exercises have been held among South African and Western naval forces. Because of the United Nations arms embargo, South Africa cannot acquire up-to-date anti-submarine war vessels or equipment.

Unlike the United States, the Soviets are not ignoring the area. They are constantly prowling the Cape with their naval forces.

During World War II, four German U-Boats, primitive craft by today's standards, sank 135 ships off the coasts of southern Africa. One modern sub could, by raiding the narrow, unprotected shipping lane, close this essential shipping route.

The United States has contingency plans to shift elements of its naval forces from the Pacific Fleet to the Indian or

Atlantic Ocean. During wartime, these ships would have to sail around the southern tip of Africa to get to their new destination, be it the Atlantic or Indian Ocean. Given the distances involved and the Soviet naval presence along both coasts of Africa, it behooves the U.S. to have friendly port facilities available to service the ships during their journey. The facts of geography make it plain that the only ports available in a time of need would be those in the Republic of South Africa.

The West continues to ignore these facts at its peril.

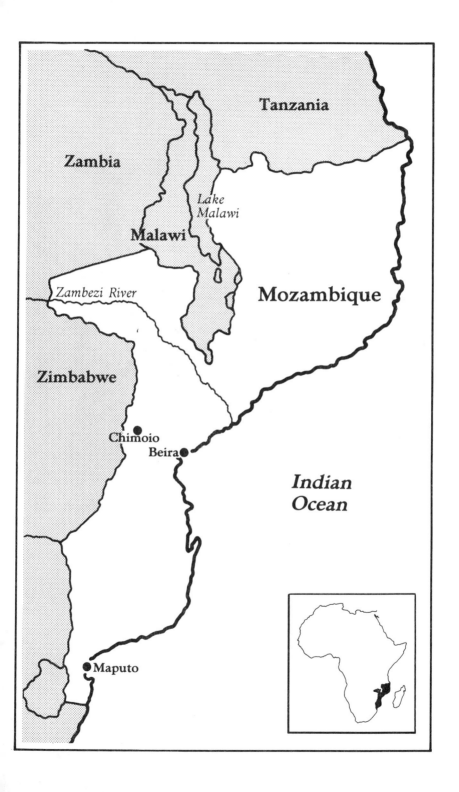

**The Fruits of Socialism—The once-thriving Mozambi-
can port of Beira is silting in as a result of over 10
years of Marxist Mozambican neglect.**

Captured Soviet 122mm mortar at RENAMO headquarters in Gorongoza. Captured Soviet-Bloc weapons and equipment are the sole means of RENAMO
supply.

60mm patrol mortar

RENAMO cavalry

4
Choke Point Control—
The Right Flank: Mozambique

On September 25, 1964, FRELIMO (Frente de Libertacao de Mocambique) began fighting in a fashion that typifies most of Africa'a anti-colonial wars. The target was not an isolated Portugese army post or remote police station. The target was an innocent Roman Catholic mission in the village of Nangololo, a town a few miles inside the Mozambican border with Tanzania. The priest, Fr. Daniel Boorman, was brutally murdered by the FRELIMO terrorists, who left his severed head on the altar of the mission. Thus began the Marxist "liberation" of Mozambique.

FRELIMO was founded in 1962 in Tanzania by Dr. Eduardo Mondlane, a professor of anthropology at Syracuse University in upstate New York. Mondlane was a Mozambican of the Shagaan tribe in southern Mozambique. Educated in South Africa, Portugal and the United States, he received his Ph.D. from Northwestern University. After earning his doctorate, Mondlane became a research officer with the United Nations Trusteeship and a lecturer in anthropology at Syracuse University.

Given encouragement, protection and support by Julius Nyerere, president of the newly independent Tanganyika, now Tanzania, Mondlane set up FRELIMO headquarters in Dar-es-Salaam where he began the military and political training of FRELIMO cadres. Training bases were established under Nyerere's protection.

The main training base was set up at Nashingwea. Other bases for FRELIMO were soon established at Kongwa, Bagumoyo and Tunduru. The arrival of Red Chinese aid to build the Tanzam Railroad, linking Dar-es-Salaam on the Indian Ocean with Lusaka, the capital of land-locked Zambia, brought with it Chinese advisors and weapons for the fledging FRELIMO guerrilla movement. Selected FRELIMO cadres were sent to guerrilla training camps in Algeria and the United Arab Republic. When the time came for FRELIMO to launch its guerrilla war against the Portuguese in Mozambique, it was better prepared and equipped than any other anti-Portuguese resistance movement in Africa.

When FRELIMO's "war of liberation" began, it was centered in the northeastern region of Mozambique, home of the war-like Makonde tribe, many of whom joined the uprising. However, the Marxist tactics of terrorism, murder, torture and selective kidnappings dampened Makonde enthusiasm.

In 1967, the guerrilla war spread to the shores of Lake Malawi, a thinly-populated area where the guerrillas could grow their food. In 1968, the terrorist war took a big step forward when FRELIMO moved into the Tete province (which abuts Zambia to the north and Rhodesia to the south) accomplishing two objectives: First, it enabled Zambian Kenneth Kaunda to provide bases and sanctuaries for FRELIMO forces; second, it allowed the Marxist terrorists to threaten the Cabora Bassa power project under construction on the Zambezi River in the heart of the Tete district. FRELIMO operations did not halt the construction of the dam, but did cut road traffic from Rhodesia to Malawi except for twice weekly convoys.

In 1969 FRELIMO was thrown into a crisis by Mondlane's assassination with a parcel bomb in Dar-es-Salaam. Although Portuguese secret police were blamed for the incident, it is widely rumored that Mondlane's successor, Samora Machel, was responsible for the fatal bomb blast. The death of Mondlane plunged FRELIMO into disarray and confusion because it was saddled with a three-headed leadership consisting of Usia Simango, Marcelino dos Santos and Samora Machel. A power struggle ensued among this triumvirate and in 1970 Samora Machel emerged as undisputed leader of FRELIMO. Machel was a hardline communist who had been trained in Algeria and the Soviet Union. The rise of Machel resulted in increased arms and support and an escalation of the war against the Portuguese.

But it was not Machel's military prowess that sealed the fate of Mozambique; rather it was an event that occurred in far-off Lisbon, the capital of Portugal. It began with a book written by a leftist general named Antonia de Spinalo. His book claimed that Portugal could not win its African wars by military means. The way out was by political capitulation in the former Portuguese colonies, which were considered overseas provinces of Portugal itself.

The Portuguese had grown tired of the long, drawn-out struggle and the price they had paid in lives and treasure was high. Many casualties were draftees who felt like foreigners in these overseas provinces. Portugal, one of the poorest countries in Europe, found the staggering cost of fighting wars a drain on the economy.

Spinalo's book struck a responsive chord in the warweary nation and triggered a left-wing revolution in Portugal. The government was tossed out by a military coup d'etat on April 25, 1974. Within three months of the coup, the leftist government of Spinalo was ready to give up Angola, Mozambique and Guinea-Bissau, each the site of much conflict. The new leftist government left no doubt in the military's mind that it was only a question of time before the Portuguese army in overseas provinces would pull out and come home.

The army's military effort quickly collapsed in Mozambique, creating a power vacuum rapidly filled by FRELIMO. Power was transferred to FRELIMO on June 25, 1975, an event that even in its wildest dreams, it didn't foresee for another ten years. Suddenly, the Republic of South Africa, the ultimate target of Soviet imperialism in Africa because of an industrial base that could finance communism in its most repressive form throughout the rest of Africa, found a communist state on one of its borders.

Within one month of taking power, Samora Machel began the disastrous ruination of the Mozambican economy. First, he nationalized schools, hsopitals, clinics and funeral parlors. Next in line were rented buildings and other private companies. Agriculture was collectivized with predictable results—output fell drastically. Machel's nationalized industries suffered severely reduced output. Freedom was rapidly diminishing under the new order in Mozambique.

Machel had planned to reorganize Mozambican society and was determined to impose his will on the hearts and minds of the people. Collectivizing agriculture was only the first step in the transformation of Mozambique to a Marxist state. Machel continued to sculpt his "new man" in Africa's premier communist showcase using the familiar communist techniques of detention and "re-education" (read: brainwashing). According to former FRELIMO minister Artur X.L. Vilankulu, "men and women were incarcerated without trial and in many cases without any sort of charges being filed against them. When the existing jails were filled, the regime began establishing what it called 're-education camps'—in reality, nothing but concentration camps. By 1984, there were thirty such camps holding more than 300,000 prisoners. . . ."[1]

Machel was following Marx to the letter, as evidenced by remarks to FRELIMO's third party congress: "The final objectives in the constitution of the People's Republic of Mozambique are, basically, the construction of the political, ideological, scientific and cultural basis of the socialist society. The constitution establishes that the land and natural resources of our country are the property of the State. It stresses the value of the collective form of production and defends the interests of the working masses. . . ."[2]

FRELIMO's totalitarian grip tightened as time went on. All private law firms were closed on the grounds that they were "incompatible with a popular system of justice."[3] The zeal to abolish all traces of private property included banning all private social clubs because they "encouraged racism, regionalism, divisionism or elitism contrary to the principles of public order as contained in the constitution."[4]

Even the U.S. State Department, which has done everything it can to help the communists in Mozambique ("wean them away" from the Soviets, they say), made a frank human rights report to Congress in 1981: "Mozambique is a one-party state controlled by FRELIMO. FRELIMO advocates a society based on Marxist-Leninist precepts. The party's membership is a small part of the total population. There is some opportunity for intraparty debate, but opposition political movements are not permitted."[5]

Despite an abundance of overtures from the State Department, including the arrangement of a meeting between President Reagan and Samora Machel at the White House and millions of dollars in loans from the U.S. Export-Import Bank and IMF, Mozambique has been drawn closer to the USSR. Soviet advisors, Cuban troops, East German secret police, Libyans, Tanzanians and Zimbabweans are working together to prop up Mozambique's communist regime. How does Mozambique pay for this "fraternal assistance"? Like their brothers in Vietnam, with slave labor. Since 1982 Machel has been forced to ship at least 11,000 young Mozambicans to East Germany as factory workers. (Our former Ambassador to Mozambique, Peter de Vos, called it "vocational training.") Once in East Germany, their passports are confiscated to prevent them from leaving.

On a personal level, the Soviet aid pact placed Machel's life in the hands of his Soviet handlers. He had a personal bodyguard of Cubans and communist East Germans who are supposedly there to protect Machel and now his successor Joaquim Chissano from so-called counter-revolutionaries. In reality, they have Soviet guns trained on Machel's head. Machel knew that his late revolutionary counterpart in Angola, Agostinho Neto, died suspiciously in a Moscow hospital. And the Soviets didn't hesitate to bump off their puppet in Afghanistan in 1978 and replace him with dictator Barbrak Karmal who himself was recently replaced (for "health reasons," they say) with Dr. Nabijullah, head of the much feared Afghan secret police.

****

What is the legacy of Marxism in Mozambique? Evo Fernandes, former Secretary General of the Mozambican National Resistance (RENAMO), said: "Mozambique in 1973 was one of the eight most economically developed countries in Africa. And we were the only one of these that did not export mineral resources, except for only a little bit of coal, tantalite and beryllium—nothing more. Mozambique was not known as a mineral exporter, and yet we were eighth in all Africa. And we were a net exporter of agricultural produce such as cotton, peanuts, sugar, tea, maize, cashews and so on. But today we belong to the dozen most underdeveloped countries in the world. The economy is completely ruined."[6]

So Machel turned to the U.S. in an effort to get bailed out. Our State Department rushed to embrace and appease the dictator: "Mozambique has undertaken a serious opening to the West in general and the United States in particular. . . . In a clear departure from past economic commitments to the Soviet bloc and Marxist economic doctrine, it has joined the IMF and World Bank, opened its doors to Western business, and moved to reinvigorate its domestic private sector, especially in agriculture."[7]

At this writing, the State Department is pushing an aid package to Mozambique. In 1985 they unsuccessfully attempted to persuade Congress to legislate military aid that would have included bringing communist Mozambican soldiers to U.S. military academies for training.

Despite these facts, Soviet military assistance to Mozambique has increased. And Machel's commitment to the USSR remains firm. It will take more than soothing words, wishful thinking and big-bank bailouts brokered by the State Department to get the Soviets out of Mozambique.

1. Tom Bethell, "State's Superfine-Tuning," *National Review* (April 19, 1985), p. 29.

2. Samora Machel, Feb. 1, 1977, in Maputo, quoted in Peter Janke, *Marxist Statecraft in Africa: What Future?* (London, England: Institute for the Study of Conflict, 1978), p. 4.

3. *Marxist Mozambique: The Question of U.S. Aid.* (Washington, D.C.: The Heritage Foundation, January 26, 1982), p. 13.

4. Ibid.

5. *Country Reports on Human Rights Practices.* Report submitted to the Committee on Foreign Relations, U.S. Senate, by the Department of State, Feb. 2, 1981 (Washington, D.C.: U.S. Government Printing Office, 1981), p. 185.

6. Interview with Secretary General Evo Fernandes, Mozambican National Resistance, in *The Journal of Defense and Diplomacy* (September 1985), p. 46.

7. Letter to the author from the State Department, March 22, 1985.

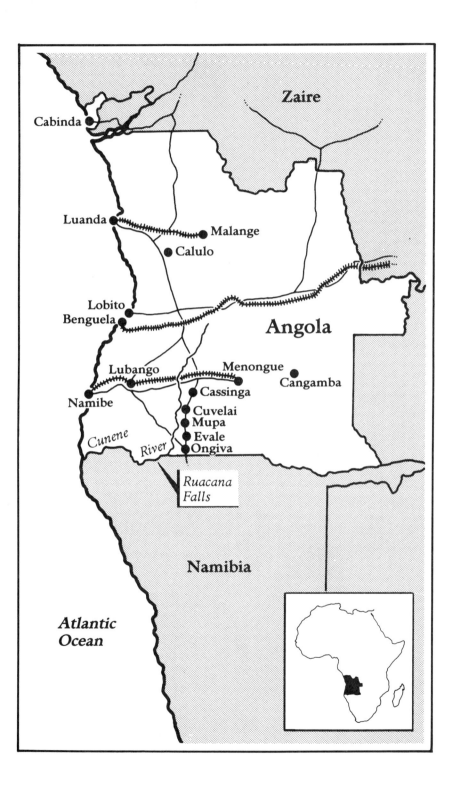

The identity papers of a Soviet advisor to SWAPO in Angola

UNITA-captured Soviet Bloc 23mm anti-aircraft gun

Soviet advisors conferring with SWAPO terrorists at a SWAPO base in Angola

Soviet advisor instructing SWAPO guerrillas in Angola

Soviet trainer conducting a sandtable training exercise at a SWAPO terrorist base in Angola.

5

Choke Point Control—
The Left Flank: Angola

The first shots in the Angolan guerrilla war against the Portuguese were fired in the capital, Luanda, on February 4, 1961 when the Luanda post office and several army and police barracks were attacked. Holden Roberto's Angolan People's Union (UPA) claimed credit for the incident.

A more serious incident occurred a few weeks later when Bakongo tribesman attacked the village of Quitexe, in the northern district of Uige, and hacked to death, with machetes, 21 Portuguese civilians. This incident touched off a revolt that during the first year killed more than 300 Portuguese and thousands of black Angolans.

The rebellion started on the northern border with the new country of Zaire, formerly the Belgian Congo, and spread south and west. However, the effects of the revolt weren't felt outside the Bakongo tribal areas sympathetic to Holden Roberto.

Roberto's liberation movement, UPA, soon became the National Front for the Liberation of Angola (FNLA). Established in 1957 in Leopoldville (now Kinsasha), it was the first of three liberation movements formed to fight against the Portuguese in the war to oust their colonial masters in the period from 1961 to 1974.

Although the FNLA fired the first shots in the armed confrontation with Portugal, it was not the oldest of the three liberation movements, which happened to be the People's Movement for the Liberation of Angola (MPLA), founded in Luanda in December 1956 by Dr. Antonio Agostinho Neto and several communist radicals of mulatto origin. Although it claimed to be the "people's party," the MPLA was limited to the mixed blood community in and around Luanda and to the Mbundu tribe whose lands were adjacent to Luanda. After several clashes with the Portuguese, the MPLA in 1963 fled to the Congo, moving to Congo-Brazzaville, where, under a new Marxist regime, its fortunes steadily improved.

In April 1964, the Chinese built a training camp for the MPLA in Bourango. From this base and others in the Congo, the MPLA infiltrated the oil-rich Cabinda province in northwestern Angola.

The independence of Zambia in 1964 also helped the MPLA. The new Zambian government permitted Neto to move some of his forces there. By early 1968, the MPLA had stationed the bulk of its force inside Zambia. They were located close to the eastern border of Angola, threatening the remote Angolan districts of Moxico and Cuanda Cubango. From sanctuaries inside Zambia, the MPLA launched short-term strikes, sometimes up to 300 kilometers in depth into the sparsely populated eastern sector in Angola.

In March 1965, Neto traveled to Moscow and returned with Soviet support. Arms and supplies began arriving at MPLA bases in Brazzaville. Neto's anointment by Moscow pushed him into the top circles of Third World radical chic.

In October the Organization of African Unity (OAU) dropped its support of Holden Roberto's FNLA and bestowed it on Neto's communist MPLA. The FNLA's base of support was drawn from the Bakongo tribe in Northern Angola. Ironically, the early chief supporter of the fledgling FNLA was a non-Bakongo Marxist politician named Patrice Lumumba. He offered to train Roberto's men and persuaded other African leaders to back his efforts.

Militarily, at this stage of the game after its initial spurt of violence that launched the colonial war, the FNLA wasn't much of a factor. It operated from bases in Zaire and limited operations to the northern Angolan-Zaire border. The Portuguese neutralized it by 1974.

In 1964, FNLA's Foreign Minister, Jonas Savimbi, became uncomfortable with the potential future of FNLA. Two years later, in March 1966, he broke with the FNLA and founded the National Union for the Total Independence of

Angola (UNITA) at Mwongai in Angola's Moxico province. At first, UNITA operated from bases in Zambia. Its guerrillas were sent into eastern Angola where they conducted their operations. UNITA lost the good will of Zambia when it sabotaged the Benguela railroad, the main route used to ship copper, Zambia's main export, to the outside world. For this transgression, Savimbi was kicked out of Zambia, spent eight months in exile in the Congo, and finally moved his command inside Angola, establishing a base in its sparsely populated region. This left him with no choice but to build his base of support with the local population in the area, which was derived largely from the Ovimbundu tribe.

Savimbi was unique among the leaders of the three factions fighting the Portuguese. Whereas Roberto and Neto operated from sanctuaries in Zaire and Brazzaville, Savimbi led UNITA from the Angolan bush. His willingness to take the same risks as his men made them loyal and determined fighters.

****

The leftist coup in Portugal on April 25, 1974, ended any further serious military effort against the three Angolan insurgency movements, just as it did in Mozambique. That July Portugal announced that it was prepared to grant independence to Angola and arranged an armistice with the three liberation movements.

On January 15, 1975, Portugal signed the Alvor Agreement with the three liberation movements; November 11, 1975, was the day Angola would gain independence. In the interim, Angola was to be ruled by a Portuguese High Commissioner and a transitional government comprised of representatives from UNITA, the FNLA and the MPLA until national elections could be held to determine which of the three movements enjoyed the political support of the majority of Angolans.

The Alvor Agreement gave equal rights and responsibilities to each of the three movements from the inauguration of the transitional government until the elected government assumed power. But as the saying goes: "The best laid schemes o' mice and men gang aft a-gley." The ink on the agreement was hardly dry before mischief began anew in Angola.

Savimbi launched a nationwide election campaign. As an accomplished orator, he was a smashing success on the hustings. In fact, polls taken in Angola during the period of March through May 1975 showed that UNITA was clearly ahead of its rivals. While Savimbi campaigned, the FNLA and MPLA prepared to fight, with the MPLA receiving tacit support from the leftist government in Portugal. In February, localized fighting broke out between the MPLA and FNLA. During March and April, Luanda was also rocked by violence between the two factions.

By May, the Alvor Agreement had been tossed aside and a series of bloody battles swept Angola as both the MPLA and FNLA jockeyed for position to crush each other. During this critical period, under pressure from the Portuguese Communist Party, the leftist government in Lisbon acted as a broker between the Soviets and MPLA. Moscow saw the geopolitical advantage and jumped into the Angolan situation with both feet. Not only had the Soviets been aiding the Marxist MPLA since October 1974, some three months prior to the Alvor Agreement, but so had East Germany, Yugoslavia, the Portuguese Communist Party and the naive Scandinavian countries. The aid was so great the MPLA had more guns than soldiers to shoot them.

This urgent preparation and arming by the MPLA should have convinced any doubters that it had no intention of abiding by any agreement signed with the other two contending liberation movements. In fact, Neto used the respite provided by the Alvor Agreement to mobilize his followers. The fighting between the MPLA and FNLA intensified with the latter eventually being driven out of Luanda.

Savimbi appealed to the two factions to end their fighting, but the transitional government issued no appeal of its own. By force of his personality, Savimbi negotiated a three-way meeting on neutral ground. Meeting in Kenya for five days beginning on June 16, 1975, the representatives agreed to resuscitate the near-dead transitional government. The result, the Nakura Agreement, established elections "sometime during October 1975."[1] Putting the agreement into practice was an exercise in futility. Within days of signing the agreement, the fighting in Angola resumed—the civil war in Angola began in earnest.

In April 1975, 200 to 300 Cuban advisers, the first of a future wave of Cuban combat troops, arrived in Angola. Fidel Castro had decided to help his fellow Marxists in Angola. By June, while the MPLA negotiated the Nakura Agreement, the Cubans were building military training centers in widely scattered areas of Angola—centers for launching military operations by the MPLA against the other two movements. The MPLA had never intended to abide by the Nakura Agreement nor to trust its destiny to any other process than force of arms.

In July the MPLA suddenly attacked UNITA, destroying any hope for a negotiated political solution. By August the situation had escalated into a full-scale civil war. Under the old theory that "my enemy's enemy is my friend," UNITA and FNLA forces were thrown together in an uneasy alliance against the MPLA.

The MPLA attacked northward from Luanda forcing the FNLA to retreat. They also pushed southward to seize the ports of Lobito, Benguela and Mocamedes (now called Namibe). Another objective of this southern communist offensive was to seize control of the Benguela railroad, a vital link for copper traveling westward from land-locked mines in Zambia to ports for shipment to the world market. Its control was important to the future Angolan economy. The MPLA's drive for control of the rail line was only partly successful. By October 1975, the communists held the western portion of the line. Its eastern portion was still in the hands of the UNITA forces.

The arrival of Cuban combat troops and massive military aid from the Soviets tipped the scale in favor of the MPLA. Neither UNITA nor the FNLA was able to match the overwhelming firepower of the communist forces. Nor were they getting much outside help, as the OAU was so deeply divided on the Angolan issue as to be completely useless.

Eventually, South Africa launched Operation Savannah,

sending small numbers of troops into Angola at the instigation, so it is said, of Dr. Henry Kissinger. This force, though small, fought well, winning a string of victories that pushed Cuban-MPLA forces back to Luanda. Unfortunately, the entry of South Africa into the fray raised a chorus of protest within the Third World. Aided by a massive propaganda effort by the left, world opinion heaped abuse on South Africa for its incursion while studiously ignoring the Cuban presence.

When the United States Senate voted in December 1975 to prohibit aid to the anti-communist factions in Angola, the South Africans realized they were "twisting slowly in the wind" and began withdrawing their troops from Angola. By March of 1976 the last South African forces marched out of Angola.

The withdrawal of western support and prohibition of any future support (the recently repealed Clark Amendment) gave the communists carte blanche in Angola. Immediately, the communists began airlifting military aid and Cuban troops. The combination enabled the Soviets to successfully intervene in Angola and to install the MPLA, while UNITA and the FNLA withdrew to the bush.

After the South African retreat, the Cubans came to Angola in droves, becoming a key element in the MPLA air force and commanding bases and sending pilots for the Soviet-supplied aircraft. They assumed key positions in the civil service and took control of political indoctrination to drum up support for the new Marxist-Leninist regime. As part of this effort, they began program planning on Angolan national radio and indoctrinating personnel to "heighten their political and ideological consciousness"; in short, to train them to become good communist propagandists.

The Union of Cuban "Journalists" also agreed to help their socialist brothers and condcuted similar indoctrination for Angolan newspaper and magazine reporters. Cuba also sent more than 700 teachers, from the Che Guevara International Teaching Detachment, whose job it was to train, take over or complement political commissars in the army and government.

In October 1976, Neto traveled to Moscow and signed two

treaties with the Soviet Union: a 20-year friendship treaty and one between the Communist Party of the Soviet Union and the MPLA. The treaties gave either the Soviet Union or the Communist Party of Russia the right to intervene in Angola when either of its interests was threatened.

Professor Dean Fourie, professor of Strategic Studies, University of South Africa at Pretoria, told the author of this book: "The treaties of friendship give the Soviets the right to intervene in Angola's affairs. For example, the treaty of friendship with Angola is in rather ambiguous language. But it provided, in the Soviets' eyes, the legalistic basis for the Soviet Union to help get either sovereignty by assisting them to eradicate colonialism, apartheid and all that sort of stuff. In those treaties, they developed legitimation for the intervention in all those countries, such as Angola, where they have treaties of friendship.

"In other words, as a hypothetical case, if Savimbi were able to overthrow the Marxist Angolan government, the Soviets would have a right to intervene and try to toss out Savimbi.

"They even have a right in Angola to start an insurrection, because they have a treaty between the two communist parties—the Soviets and Angola—as well as between the two governments.

"Thus they have the right to intervene to restore the government, which is the Angolan Communist Party. This is very much an extension of the Brezhnev doctrine.

"This does not hold for all countries. They don't have interparty treaties everywhere like they do in Angola. But where they do, they feel they have legitimated Soviet intervention. This is always open to interpretation, which the Soviets use, depending on the circumstances at the time.

"What does this mean in the real world? This means that if anyone were to try and overthrow the government, which is supported by the Soviet Union, even if an internal party was trying to restore democracy in a country in Africa or one of the island states as are certain parts of Asia, the Soviet Union could intervene and prevent it. They could do this even if the government involved had no time to ask them for their assistance.

"If there were an uprising in one of these countries and the Soviet Union decided that it was in its interest to support the uprising, they could also intervene and support the uprising, which is what they virtually did in Afghanistan.

"But look at the way they interpreted their intervention in Afghanistan. They claimed they were called in to assist in virtually restoring order which, according to them, they had a perfect right to do under the terms of the treaties they had with both the Afghanistan government and the Afghanistan Communist Party.

"As you can see, they use those treaties and interparty relations to do a variety of things, but always with the view of furthering the interests of the Soviet Union."[2]

The Angolan security service was set up along the lines of the Cuban secret police and was controlled by the Cuban intelligence service, the DGI. The DGI, in turn, is tightly controlled by the Soviet KGB. Angola was shortly designated by the MPLA as a "Marxist-Leninist Republic" to be ruled by a "democratic revolutionary dictatorship"—the usual jargon used to cover totalitarian ambitions.

The new People's Republic of Angola abolished private property and set about the nationalization of the Angolan economy. In 1977, a new currency was introduced along with new regulations restricting the amount allowed to be converted from the old to the new. The goal of this action, as MPLA officials freely admitted, was to destroy the middle class in Angola.

Meanwhile, Soviet surrogates continued to pour into the new Russian colony. Nineteen thousand Cuban military troops were in Angola along with 10,000 Cuban civilians or political cadres. The Soviet bloc didn't restrict itself to merely furnishing warm human bodies to act as the MPLA's Praetorian Guard. They sent tons of military equipment to Angola. By 1978 almost $500 million worth of arms and other military equipment had been sent by the Soviet bloc. Near the end of the decade, in addition to the Cubans, 5,500 Soviet soldiers and/or advisors were training FAPLA (People's Armed Forces for the Liberation of Angola) soldiers. In addition to their duties as trainers, the Soviets were exercising actual military control in FAPLA down to the company level.

East Germans showed up to train the internal security apparatus of the MPLA government. By 1979 5,000 East Germans had arrived in Angola. Other Iron Curtain nations added another 15,000 personnel, all under the control and guidance of Moscow. The Soviets were in firm control of their far-flung African colony. This was a huge investment on the part of Moscow in an area far from its homeland. There was a difference between Moscow's "benevolent aid" to its colonies and Western aid given to Third World countries. Moscow makes its colonies pay for the arms and equipment. By the end of the 1970's the Soviets were spending more than $2 million per day on Angola, none of it helping the Angolan economy.

Angola is a country with tremendous economic potential. It has a wealth of minerals, oil and much arable land. Angola could be an economic power on the African continent, but will never become one as long as it remains a Marxist state. Only one exportable product has saved the Angolan communist dictatorship—oil produced by the Chevron oil subsidiary, Cabinda-Gulf, operating in Cabinda province. The concern is jointly owned by Chevron through its Gulf subsidiary (49 percent) and Sonangol, the Angolan national oil company (51 percent). The operation earns the MPLA regime about $2 billion per year in taxes and royalties, 60 percent of which pays for Soviet military hardware and 35,000 occupation troops currently stationed in Angola. Castro is earning about $480 million per year from the deal, or about $1,000 per month per soldier.

Neto began to realize that the Soviets would never supply economic aid to bail out his failing economy, so early in 1977 he began making noises as if he were trying to become independent from the Soviets, hoping to get Western aid. This alarmed radical elements in the MPLA. Officers in the 8th Armored Brigade, backed by the KGB, began plotting a coup to oust Neto. Neto discovered the plot and crushed it.

All was not lost for those who wanted to see Neto go. In September 1979, he died undergoing surgery in Moscow. Rumor had it that he was murdered by the Soviets because he was getting too independent. Within 24 hours of Neto's death, Jose Eduardo dos Santos was "elected" president of Angola and commander-in-chief of FAPLA by the central committee of the MPLA. Dos Santos is a Soviet lackey. After joining the MPLA in the late fifties, he went to Russia in 1961 and earned a degree in petroleum engineering from the Baku Petroleum and Gas Institute. As a student in the Soviet Union, Dos Santos caught the eye of the KGB and became a leading political organizer of Third World students studying there. After graduation, he took a one-year course in military communications, a strange post-graduate course for a petroleum engineer.

When Dos Santos returned to Angola he made it plain he wasn't going to be searching for oil. He rejoined his MPLA comrades fighting the Portuguese and handled communications on the northern front. He moved into the party hierarchy and soon switched to diplomacy. A close ally of Neto, Dos Santos became Minister of External Affairs after the MPLA seized power in 1975 and finagled Angola's way into the OAU. After a long struggle, he procured U.N. membership for Marxist Angola.

In any dictatorship, there are political sharks hanging around waiting for the leader to slip up so they can get rid of him. As they say, the king is usually killed by his court. For his own good, political as well as personal, Dos Santos does what the Soviets tell him to do. He is threatened by Soviet-controlled MPLA party members keeping a close watch on him so he won't stray from Moscow's line. Men like Ambrosia Lukaki, Lucio Lara and Angolan Air Force General Icca Carerria (also a general in the Soviet army) represent powerful claimants to Do Santos's throne.

****

Today, the Soviets, with naval facilities in Luanda, are in a position to interdict shipping passing around the Cape of Good Hope up the west coast of Africa toward Europe or heading across the South Atlantic for South or North America. Angola would serve as an unsinkable aircraft carrier in the South Atlantic, much as Cuba serves the same purpose in the Caribbean.

The Angolan ports of Luanda, Lobito and Namibe allow

the Soviets to import vast quantities of military supplies to Angola that are used not only by FAPLA, but communist revolutionaries such as SWAPO (in Namibia) or the ANC (in South Africa). Between 1984 and 1985, the Soviets amassed $2 billion worth of advance military hardware in Angola, including 1,000 battle tanks, more than 100 advanced MIG jet fighters, long range strategic bombers (TU-95) and MI-24 HIND D helicopter gunships, a weapon our Defense Department calls a 'flying tank." Clearly, the Soviets are pre-positioning forces in preparation for the military conquest of sub-Saharan Africa.

1. Charles Moser, *Combat on Communist Territory* (Washington, D.C.: Free Congress Foundation, 1985), p. 78.

2. Interview with Professor Dean Fourie, University of South Africa, Pretoria, by the author, May 1984.

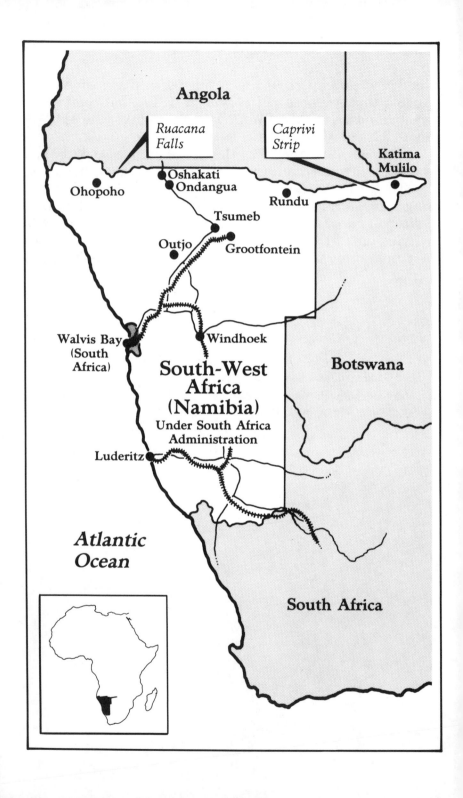

A mounted-infantry patrol of the South West African Territorial Force (SWATF) searches for SWAPO terrorists in the sweltering sandy bush of Ovamboland in SWA/Namibia.

**Clearing a SWAPO-planted landmine in SWA/
Namibia. Landmines are one of the terrorist's
favorite weapons.**

SWAPO terrorism at work. On April 15, 1984, two American diplomats were killed by a SWAPO bomb planted in a civilian gas station in Oshakati, SWA/ Namibia.

Bushman trackers from 201 Battalion, SWATF, follow SWAPO terrorist tracks in Ovamboland. These trackers have tracked and followed the terrorist spoor for over 200 kilometers before catching and killing the terrorists.

Helicopters are vital weapons in the war against terrorism in SWA/Namibia.

The troops take a break from the hot, dusty patrol.

6

Encircling The Republic Of
South Africa—SWA/Namibia

The seeds of the current South West Africa/Namibia (hereafter, Namibia) controversy took root in World War I when Namibia, then South West Africa, was a German colony. In 1915 South Africa, as one of the Allied Nations, invaded and conquered South West Africa in the name of the British crown and continued to administer it under military occupation until 1920. Then the League of Nations awarded South Africa a class "C" mandate over South West Africa, under which South Africa could administer the territory as an "integral" part of its own territory. This it did for the next 25 years until the end of World War II, when the League of Nations was disbanded and the United Nations was founded. Since its inception, the UN has worked vigorously to end South Africa's administration of Namibia and place the country under UN trusteeship.

In fact, when a series of actions taken before the International Court of Justice to stop South Africa's administration of the country failed in 1966, the General Assembly adopted a resolution claiming to terminate the League of Nation's mandate. Despite this resolution, South Africa continued to administer Namibia, and in 1978, agreed to grant Namibia independence.

****

SWAPO, the South West African People's Organization, was founded in Cape Town in 1957 by a former railway policeman, Herman Toivo. Originally called the Owambo-

land People's Congress, SWAPO became the Owamboland
People's Organization and finally the South West Africa
People's Organization. Name changes were made to disguise
the organization's tribal base when dealing with international supporters and also to attract members from other tribal
groups.

SWAPO initially exploited grievances among the Owambos concerning migrant labor policies, changing the tribal
headman system, independence for Namibia and finally, the
key issue for SWAPO, majority rule. Given the demographics
of Namibia, this would amount to neverending Owambo
control.

The population of Namibia is a little more than one
million. It is, however, a heterogeneous population with
twelve different ethnic groups, none constituting a majority.
They are in order of size, Owambo, nearly 50 percent of the
population, White, Damra, Herero, Kavango, Nama, Colored,
East Caprivian, Bushmen, Rehobath Baster, Kaokolander,
and Tswana. Each has its own language, or languages,
except the Damra, who speak Nama and Herero. The Owambo comprise seven distinct tribes and use two written languages. The Whites speak Afrikaans, German and English.

SWAPO is an Owambo-based organization whose terrorist activities are meant to intimidate fellow tribesmen.

By 1962, disappointed by its lack of political success,
SWAPO decided more radical measures were necessary to
impose its will on Namibia, and so it created a military wing,
the People's Liberation Army of Namibia (PLAN). Force
would be SWAPO's vehicle to grab power in the independent
Namibia. After embarking on this course, SWAPO sought
and obtained the support and sponsorship of Soviet bloc
communist states which lavished huge quantities of arms
and equipment on their new comrades. SWAPO terrorists
were trained in the fine arts of murder, terror and intimidation by scores of Soviet and Soviet-bloc advisors.

This support is well-documented. In November 1982
testimony before the Subcommittee on Security and Terrorism, chaired by Senator Jeremiah Denton (R-AL), clearly
showed that SWAPO receives extensive Soviet aid and is, in
effect, Soviet controlled:

"... Dr. [Chester] Crocker [Assistant Secretary of State for African Affairs] indicated in his testimony that the administration estimates that SWAPO receives about 90 percent of its military support and 60 percent of its overall support from communist sources. Advocate Jeriertundo Kozonguinzi also drew the subcommittee's attention to the scale of the Soviet bloc's commitment to SWAPO, pointing to the large quantities of weapons and military equipment made available in Angola. The younger witnesses, Mr. Namolo and Mr. Hashiko, testified about their training in Angola by Soviet instructors. They also described their indoctrination in the Soviet Union in 'socialism and communism, Leninist teachings and political economy.'

"Documents submitted for the record contain evidence of the training of large numbers of SWAPO 'cadres' in the Soviet Union both in military doctrines and, without exception, in Marxist-Leninist ideology. The position of 'political commissar' is entrenched at all organization levels of SWAPO. These men, selected on the basis of their educational attainments and understanding of ideology, are trained at the KOMSO-MOL Party School in the Soviet Union, in the German Democratic Republic and in Cuba. Documents confirming this have been included in the report.

"On the basis both of the testimony presented and the documents made available to the subcommittee, the conclusion is inescapable that the Soviets and their communist allies within SWAPO ensure that Marxist-Leninist doctrine is systematically taught to all who are recruited for, or pressed into service in SWAPO and PLAN.

"The tragedy of this is illuminated by the testimony of Mr. Andreas Shipango. He was founder of SWAPO in 1960, and in 1958 of its predecessor, the Ovambo People's Organization (OPO). He testified that the movement was not created as a communist party or as a front for the communists and that the chief ally of the OPO in its struggle for the rights of the people of Namibia was the Liberal Party of South Africa. He testified that the South African Communist Party was originally hostile to the OPO and to SWAPO. Mr. Shipanga stated that it was only after his arrest and that of his followers in April 1976 that the Political Program was altered to provide for the reconstitution of SWAPO as an organization espousing Marxist-Leninist principles. "The purpose of these hearings was not to debate U.S. policy toward southern Africa. ... Our purpose has been to determine, through testimony of witnesses and the evaluation of documents, the extent to which the Soviet Union has successfully influenced, penetrated, or come to control the African National Congress, the South West African People's Organization, and other national liberation movements in southern Africa, such as FRELIMO. Our purpose has been to examine more closely the Soviet ties with terrorism in southern Africa.

"The evidence received by the subcommittee is deeply disturbing. It suggests strongly that the original purposes of the ANC and SWAPO have been subverted, and that the Soviets and their allies have achieved alarming effective control over them. The demonstrated activities of these organizations, moreover, cannot easily be reconciled with the goal of liberation or the promotion of freedom. The evidence has thus served to illustrate once again the Soviet Union's support for terrorism under the guise of aiding struggles for national liberation. It is past time to bring these facts to the attention of policy-makers, the American people, and the world at large."[1]

The terror campaign of SWAPO was launched in February 1966 at Ondumbashe in Owamboland near the Namibian-Angolan border. Two shops were plundered and the shopkeepers, a Portuguese and an Owambo, were murdered. Other incidents of a similar nature followed quickly: an attack on the village of Oshikango in September, the mugging of two Owambo chiefs in November, a raid on another chief's office in December that resulted in the murder of one of the chief's bodyguards, and an attack on a farm in the Grootfontein area.

These attacks bore the classic stamp of a Soviet-directed terror campaign. The main targets are not those who can fight back—soldiers or policemen—but tribal leaders, the headmen and their families, as well as shopkeepers and other helpless civilians. The brunt of the suffering at the hands of the self-proclaimed "liberators" has been borne by the ordinary Owambo citizen, who risks being murdered, kidnapped or blown up by land mines on the road.

But all was not well for the Marxist terrorists led by Sam Nujoma; local Owambos were not supporting their would-be liberators. The local population was not responding to the tactics of murder and intimidation. The more SWAPO tried, the less backing it received from the so-called oppressed masses of Namibia.

In 1973, SWAPO successfully enforced its call for a boycott of the general elections in Owamboland. Only 2.7 percent braved SWAPO's threats of violence and went out to vote. Yet, two years later, after accelerating terrorist activity, SWAPO's call for a boycott of the 1975 election was a failure.

SWAPO had better luck in the international arena of politics than it did on the battlefield or among the people of Namibia. In 1976, SWAPO was declared by the UN as the sole "authentic representative of the Namibian people."[2] In the same resolution, the General Assembly supported SWAPO "in their struggle, by all means, including armed struggle, to achieve self-determination, freedom and national independence."[3] This declaration was both a financial boon and propaganda victory for SWAPO. The UN, through various organs, allocated at least $40 million in aid to SWAPO between 1977-1981. The U.S., with taxpayer dollars, contributes about 30 percent of this total. SWAPO uses these funds to feed, clothe, educate and train its terrorists. UN funds are also used by SWAPO to train its cadres as government functionaries for the future, if and when SWAPO "liberates"-Namibia.

Under UN Resolution 34/92F (1979), SWAPO is guaranteed free publicity provided by the UN Department of Public Information of the Secretariat "to intensify the wide-spread and continuous dissemination of information on the struggle for liberation being waged by the people of Namibia, guided by the liberation movement, the SWAPO."[4] Thus, SWAPO has an exclusive avenue, denied other Namibian political entities, to disseminate its Marxist propaganda throughout the world using the UN distribution network.

In 1981, *The New York Times* revealed that SWAPO was

using UN refugee camps to train and recruit guerrillas. Bernard Nossiter reported that camps in Angola, designed for 10,000 Namibian school children on a coffee plantation 200 miles south of Luanda, were training students "to return as guerrillas" to Namibia. The students ranged from 5 to 18 years old, "most of them well under 16."

Nossiter reported that daily use of the camp's resources were in the hands of SWAPO and that it was easy for the terror group to deceive the UN about the camp's purpose since UN representatives only visited about once per month. As Nossiter was leaving the camp, he and departing visitors were serenaded by a choral group chanting the following: "We are determined that Namibia must be free. Marxism-Leninism is our ideology, founded on scientific socialism."[5] U.S. taxpayers provide 25 percent of the money going to this camp.

In short, force and violence are the trademark of SWAPO. Even its apologists in the West cannot deny this. SWAPO's capo, Sam Nujoma, made this point quite clear in a February 28, 1978, television interview in which he warned viewers that when SWAPO came to power, the "people" (SWAPO terrorists) will do away with "traitors," including the police and armed forces, and "puppets" belonging to some 45 other political parties in Namibia. Nujoma's goals for Namibia are clear: "The question of black majority rule is out. We are not fighting for majority rule. We are fighting to seize power in Namibia for the benefit of the Namibian people. We are revolutionaries."[6]

The Portuguese downfall in Angola in 1974 was a blessing for SWAPO. Instead of Portuguese pressure and hostility, SWAPO was given bases and sanctuary by the MPLA and Soviets in Angola, just north of their target areas—the Owambo tribal lands in Namibia. Massive aid and Eastern block instructors swept into the SWAPO camps, bringing with them a plague of terrorism in the Owambo tribal area. And borrowing a page from Israeli history, South African security forces launched cross-border strikes in Owamboland on SWAPO bases.

In May 1978 South Africa conducted coordinated airborne and mechanized strikes against widely separated

SWAPO bases in Angola. One was at least 250 kilometers inside the country. SWAPO suffered devastating losses: 1,000 killed and 200 captured. This loss of trained terrorists was a blow from which SWAPO has yet to recover. It forced SWAPO to spread out surviving forces and mix them with larger numbers of raw recruits, which led to such a drop in their effectiveness that by the end of 1979 SWAPO losses exceeded their recruiting rate.

Additionally, SWAPO was no longer safe inside Angola and was forced to change its strategy; it could no longer move large groups of terrorists southward to target areas without risking an attack by security forces. Now SWAPO terrorists move to the border in groups numbering 50 or 60 men. When they reach the border, they split into smaller groups of less than a dozen. The targets are still tribal leaders, politicians, teachers and shopkeepers as well as their families. In addition, the terrorists indiscriminately place land mines. A SWAPO mine planted in a gas station in Oshakati killed two American diplomats on April 15, 1984.

SWAPO, however, has lost much of its initial effectiveness. A look at the numbers of its forces suggests why. In 1978, SWAPO forces numbered 16,000. By 1984, the number had dwindled to 6,700. In short, SWAPO had taken 10,000 casualties in a seven-year period—and they are casualties that have yet to be replaced by recruits. SWAPO terrorism in Namibia has been contained.

Only the UN and the U.S. State Department can help SWAPO now. UN Security Council resolution 435, supported by our State Department, calls for UN supervised, one-man, one-vote elections to determine who will rule an independent Namibia. But since the UN has granted SWAPO official observer status and recognizes the terrorist organization as the "sole and authentic representative" of the Namibian people, it already enjoys quasi-recognition as the government of Namibia. SWAPO's status as a UN observer is shared by the PLO and ANC.

More recently, the State Department has tried to negotiate independence for Namibia by linking South Africa's implementation of UN resolution 435 to the withdrawal of Cuban forces from Angola. As recently as March 1986, South

Africa took a first step toward Namibian independence by agreeing to implement resolution 435 by August 1, 1986, if Angola would agree to a withdrawal of 35,000 Cuban forces. The MPLA communists rejected the plan. It is unlikely that all Cuban forces will ever leave Angola, since at least 17,000 Cubans were given Angolan citizenship to sidestep just such an agreement for withdrawal and Namibian independence. Chester Crocker, Assistant Secretary of State for African Affairs, has admitted that his negotiations do not include Cuban military "advisors" or civilian personnel, and no provisions are being considered for the removal of other Soviet-bloc personnel.

In view of the financial aid and observer status granted to SWAPO by the UN, just how fair could any future UN supervised election be? Could UN representatives be impartial observers? All knowledgeable analysts in South Africa and the United States know that SWAPO will win a UN-sponsored election, if for no other reason than that people want to support whom they perceive to be the winner. They have been told by the U.N. that, indeed, SWAPO, whether they like it or not, is their "sole, authentic representative."

UN control of the machinery for Namibian independence would spell the end of freedom in Namibia—the UN would surely turn the country over to the bloody, Marxist thugs that compose SWAPO. If that happens, South Africa will be, with the exception of Botswana, facing Soviet-controlled colonies on all its border. Thus would the Soviet-Mongol encirclement of South Africa be complete.

1. Report of the Chairman of the Subcommittee on Security and Terrorism, op. cit., pp. 19-20.
2. U.N. Resolution 31/146, para. 2.
3. Ibid.
4. *How the U.N. Aids Marxist Guerrilla Groups* (Washington, D.C.: The Heritage Foundation, April 8, 1982, p. 11.
5. Ibid.
6. Willem Steenkamp, *Borderstrike* (Stoneham, Mass.: Butterworth Publishers, 1983), p. 9.

A SWATF base camp in Ovamboland, SWA/Namibia

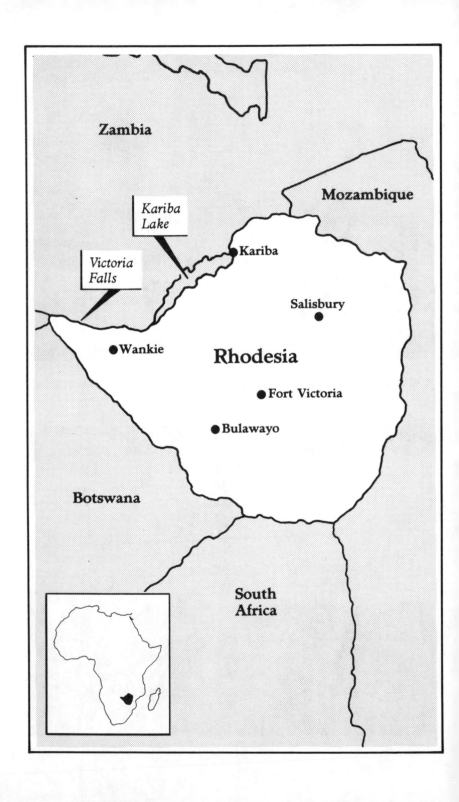

7
Rhodesia

Rhodesia was the creation of a wealthy British megalomaniac, Cecil John Rhodes, who amassed his vast fortune in the diamond and gold fields of South Africa and dreamed of extending British dominion from the Cape of Good Hope north to the Nile delta in Egypt. Fueled by tales that the fabled riches of King Solomon lay in the territory between the Limpopo and Zambezi rivers, Rhodes secured the Rudd mining concession from Lobenguela, king of the Ndebele nation that ruled the territory where the legendary mines supposedly lay. With this mining concession, Rhodes wheedled a Royal Charter out of the British government granting the authority to set up a new colony in the area that would be ruled by a private company, Rhodes' British Africa company (BSA).

In 1890 Rhodes sent several hundred well-armed men into the area to establish his authority. Lobenguela threatened to unleash his warriors on the Pioneers, as the men were called, but backed down after he saw the modern firepower of the white man.

Although the first settlers didn't find the pot of gold at the end of the rainbow and faced many lean years, their quest for the storied gold deposits continued. In 1893, the BSA contrived a war against Lobenguela's warriors, claiming the Ndebele were the aggressors. Lured by the promises of farms and mining claims, columns of well-armed settlers raced toward Lobengula's capital in Gubulawayo, which was captured and razed after the Ndebele put up token resistenace. Lobengula fled north into the bush with patrols of the victorious settlers in hot pursuit. He died before he was caught.

The victorious settlers received the farms and mining concessions they came for; even the vast Ndebele cattle herds were parcelled out as spoils of war. The BSA built a new town called Bulawayo over the ruins of the Ndebele capital. Thus, Rhodesia was born in a spasm of colonial brigandage energized by the preeminent freebooter of the British Empire, Cecil Rhodes.

Rhodes, by then Prime Minister of the Cape Colony, one of two British possessions within the confines of the present-day Republic of South Africa (the other was Natal on the Indian Ocean coast of South Africa), still faced obstacles blocking the way to realizing his dream of making a corridor of British possessions from the Cape north to Cairo. Two Boer republics, the Orange Free State and Transvaal, lay between Cape Colony and his new domain of Rhodesia (Rhodes had modestly allowed the new land to be named after him.) He thought the two holdouts must be shown the benefits of British imperial rule before he could march north from Rhodesia to the Nile.

That part of Rhodes's wealth was derived from the gold fields of the Rand located in heart of the Transvaal, a Boer republic, was a source of irritation he planned to remove. Seeking to exploit the complaints and hardships of the English-speaking community in Johannesburg, Rhodes planned his biggest, most audacious act of piracy—to seize control of the Transvaal and overthrow its government, led by Rhodes antagonist President Paul Kruger.

Rhodesia would be used as the launching pad for Rhodes's secret plan to seize the Transvaal. The attack had to be made secretly to prvent intervention by the British government, for while the Crown may have admired Rhodes and shared his imperial fantasies, the two Boer republics were legitimate states; even the British couldn't turn a blind eye while one of their colonial officials invaded another sovereign state. So Rhodes's plan hinged on deception and secrecy—a contrived uprising by "oppressed" British miners in Johannesburg and an armed intervention by BSA company forces to protect them.

On December 29, 1895, the BSA forces, some 600-strong, led by Rhodes's right-hand man Dr. Leander Starr Jameson, crossed the border into the Transvaal and the notorious Jameson Raid was on. Unfortunately, the scheme quickly turned into a fiasco—Kruger's commandos cut the raiders to pieces and captured them with evidence incriminating Rhodes. Rhodes, the BSA company and the British government were humiliated by the event.

Jameson's fiasco also had disastrous effects in Rhodesia. It had stripped the colony of most of its armed forces, who were either dead or languishing in prisons in the Transvaal, and left Rhodesia open to attack by black natives who rose in revolt. The revolt lasted 18 months and was finally put down by the remaining settlers, reinforced by British troops.

Although Rhodes's role in the Jameson affair cost him the prime ministership of the Cape Colony, his wealth and influence were enough to keep him out of prison. Nor did the British government revoke the royal charter enjoyed by the BSA company as punishment for the Jameson raid.

Thus, Rhodesia was born amid strife and gunsmoke. It would end in similar fashion.

Rather than revoke the BSA charter, the British government sent a representative in the person of Lord Grey to keep an eye on the Rhodesians. Grey and his successors had little luck with the independent-minded Rhodesians who, taking their cue from Rhodes, easily manipulated the British government and its representatives. They thought Britain had no part in founding the country, didn't help it through its difficult, early years, and hadn't done anything for it since. Rhodesians, at least the whites, didn't think the charter gave a small island nation 6,000 miles away the right to poke its nose into their affairs. So the British kept a low profile and allowed them to run things as they saw fit. Still, the Rhodesians were loyal supporters of the Empire, making significant contributions and sacrifices on behalf of Britain in all of her 20th-century wars.

Throughout this period, Rhodesia acted as if it were an independent country. In 1923, a referendum was held in Rhodesia to decide whether it would adopt home rule or become part of the Union of South Africa. Rhodesia chose home rule and as a result, the British government granted Rhodesia the right to legislate, maintain an army and run the civil government, all of which the Rhodesians had been doing unofficially since the colony was formed. Britain retained the power of legislative veto and responsibility for foreign affairs and "native" legislation, although it never exercised them.

****

World War II did irreparable damage to the British Empire. Exhausted by the long costly war and economically weak, Britain began the process of decolonization, which threatened white rule in many of its colonies.

But the whites of Central Africa were determined to resist the winds of change buffeting the continent. A last ditch attempt to maintain the status quo was the Federation of Rhodesias (Northern [now Zambia] and Southern [now Zimbabwe]) and Nyasaland. The Federation had a short life of ten years between its founding in 1953 and its breakup in 1963. The whites had hoped to use the Federation to perpetuate their rule. It had the opposite effect, as black nationalist leaders emerged in each of the three Federation states: Kenneth Kaunda in Northern Rhodesia, Joshua Nkomo in Southern Rhodesia, and Dr. Hastings Banda in Nyasaland.

The Federation broke up and blacks became leaders in two of the three countries—Kuanda in the new nation of Zambia and Banda in Malawi, the former Federation member Nyasaland. In the third country, Rhodesia, the whites were determined to continue ruling.

In 1964 the election of two leaders, one in Rhodesia and the other in Great Britain, brought the crisis to a head. Ian Douglas Smith became Prime Minister of Rhodesia and the socialist Harold Wilson was elected Prime Minister of Great Britain.

The conservative Smith and socialist Wilson didn't see eye to eye on anything. Wilson was determined not to grant independence to Rhodesia unless majority rule was guaranteed. Meanwhile Smith declared there would be no African nationalist government in Rhodesia in his lifetime. Grave errors of judgment and sheer arrogance on Wilson's part, fueled by emotionalism, were the hallmark of their negotiations and decisions. Threats, counterthreats and plain old bluff were the tools they used against each other. Yet on one item, Smith was not bluffing. He had been elected Prime Minister by promising his fellow Rhodesians that he would cut Rhodesia's colonial bonds, unilaterally if necessary, if pushed too far by the arrogant Wilson.

Wilson thought Smith was bluffing. He wasn't. On November 11, 1965, at the eleventh hour of the eleventh day of the eleventh month—a reminder to the world of Rhodesia's past and proud war record—Ian Smith and Rhodesia declared Unilateral Declaration of Independence (UDI). It was the first rebellion against the Crown since the American War for Independence.

Wilson's answer was economic sanctions, a move predicated on an overestimation of the effects of trade sanctions against Rhodesia and an underestimation of its people's ability to overcome them. Britain first imposed economic sanctions, then an oil embargo. Then the U.N. joined in, ordering a total ban on trade with Rhodesia. Far from bringing Rhodesia to her knees, from 1969-1974—before a world recession and the fall of Mozambique to the communists—Rhodesia's economic growth outstripped Britain's. Wilson and his successors had not counted on the ingenuity of the Rhodesians, who made or grew essentials they couldn't acquire from the outside world. Rhodesia became self-sufficient.

The Rhodesians easily overcame U.N. sanctions; trade with her black-ruled northern neighbors, as well as the West, flourished. Many African states ignored the sanctions completely. In fact, most members of the Organization of African Unity, which were loud in their condemnation of Rhodesia, traded with her. As President Bongo of Gabon once said: "If I do not give a list, it is out of courtesy." The situation was rife with hypocrisy. The black states vociferously condemned white racism, but were the first to trade with its progenitors. Rhodesian beef and South African wine were served on the tables of African presidential palaces. Rhodesian corn fed thousands of black Africans, including those determined to see the end of white rule there.

UDI, however, set in motion a sequence of events that would change the map of Africa once again. British and

American politicians would come and go, searching for a solution to the situation. It would be 14 long years before the rebellion was over and majority rule imposed. And when it was, the incoming government would be far worse than anything the principal players in the political arena could have imagined. It killed 30,000 Rhodesians; thousands more were injured or maimed before a shaky peace came and a new nation, Zimbabwe, slowly rose from the swirling ashes and gunsmoke.

In the mid 1960s, the prospects for African nationalists were bleak. The leaders of the nationalist movement in Rhodesia—Joshua Nkomo, Ndabaningi Sithole, Robert Mugabe and others—were languishing in prison. Nkomo's party, the Zimbabwe African People's Union (ZAPU) and his rival, Sithole's Zimbabwe African National Union (ZANU), had been banned. Officers who weren't in jail had fled the country.

UDI had forced the black nationalists to the violent forceful overthrow of the ruling whites. They looked first to Britain to act for them. But Britain refused to take up arms.

The black nationalists' first efforts didn't promise much success. The Rhodesian security forces easily destroyed ZAPU and ZANU guerrillas who had infiltrated Rhodesia from bases in Zambia and areas in Mozambique that were controlled by communist insurgents trying to overthrow the Portuguese government. As expected, the communist world rushed to embrace the guerrilla groups, giving supplies and trainers. The Chinese and Soviets vied with each other to take the guerrilla movements under wing, each convinced that its brand of communism was the correct model to follow. The Chinese could supply aid and instruction, but not on a scale with that of the Soviets.

The Soviets could not only supply arms, money and "scholarships" to terrorist training schools in the Soviet Union, but could call upon their surrogates throughout their colonial empire to provide mercenaries and/or advisors to the guerrilla movements. For example, the Russians called on the communist East Germans to organize secret police units and establish a Soviet-controlled underground communications network. And as a last resort, the Cubans could be rushed in to tip the balance in favor of the Soviet-backed guerrilla movement, as they had in Angola and Ethiopia.

Actions such as these allowed the Soviets to emerge as the main benefactor of African "national liberation movements" in the 1960s and 1970s. But the aforementioned facts notwithstanding, it was the Chinese-backed ZANU movement of Robert Mugabe that eventually won power in Rhodesia.

The initial weakness of Rhodesian communist guerrillas made it hard for the Soviets to control them. They quarrelled more among themselves than they fought against white rule. In fact, they had to be separated in Rhodesian prisons: the Nkomo men in Gonadudringwa and the Sithole men in Wha Wha. Exiled leaders were equally impotent. Faced with the armed might of Rhodesia's Security Forces, they could only sulk in Tanzania or Lusaka and do little else but eat, drink and boast about victories in some distant future. They didn't seem anxious to hurry back to the front lines to assist their struggling comrades. Their lack of zeal for actual combat prompted Zambian President Kenneth Kaunda to call them "chicken-in-the-basket" soldiers. When they did muster the courage to fight, it was against each other.

The OAU and the Presidents of Tanzania and Zambia, the so-called confrontation states, tried constantly to get the guerrillas to stop their feuding and form a joint political and military command. Their efforts resulted in the formation of the Patriotic Front in October 1976, a very shaky alliance of factions: ZAPU, led by Joshua Nkomo, and ZANU, led by Robert Mugabe. (Mugabe had been ZANU's secretary general when Sithole was its leader. However, after Mugabe's release from Wha Wha prison in 1974, he consolidated his power and became ZANU's new leader.)

The alliance between Nkomo and Mugabe was nothing more than a public relations ploy to give their left-liberal supporters in the West a device for showing solidarity with these so-called freedom fighters. Reality was a different matter. The more arms each wing received, the more inclined they were to turn them on each other, a situation easily and often exploited by the Rhodesians. Sometimes the Security Forces would inform one of the groups about the other's location, sit back, and let them fight each other. On other

occasions, one guerrilla force would inform the Security
Forces as to the location of their rivals and let the army
launch a pre-emptive strike on their rival.

This internecine warfare was fueled by differences over
ideology and tribal alligiance, with the rivalry between the
Soviet and Chinese only adding to an already explosive
situation.

Nkomo's forces, based primarily in Zambia, and heavily
supplied by the Soviets, were built as a conventional force.
Nkomo's dream was to march into Salisbury, leading his
conquering army. Mugabe's forces, based in Mozambique and
Tanzania, waged guerrilla warfare along the classic Maoist
lines. The abdication of Mozambique by the Portuguese in
1974 proved to be a big boost to ZANU's fortunes, since
Mugabe was able to train a large number of guerrillas there
under the protection of the new communist regime.

From these bases, Mugabe sent guerrillas into the huge
Tribal Trust Lands, areas reserved for the exclusive use of
black Rhodesian tribes, to build up his ZANU political
infrastructure within Rhodesia. After much training and
indoctrination, Mugabe's men would infiltrate Rhodesia to
operate in the classic mode of guerrilla warfare. The guerrillas
used an "oil-patch" approach to their warfare, putting their
strength and organization into the Tribal Trust Lands, from
which they slowly spread out to other areas. Once safe havens
were established among the subverted population, military
operations were conducted against governmental infrastruc-
tures in the Tribal Trust Lands—the chiefs, teachers, civil
workers, etc.—or against neighboring white farmers. Mugabe's forces bore the brunt of the fighting. When the December
1979 ceasefire came, there were more than 17,000 ZANU
guerrillas inside Rhodesia.

Nkomo's forces also launched guerrilla attacks, primarily from bases in Zambia and Botswana. But, reflecting the
thinking of their Soviet advisors, ZAPU was building up for
conventional force invasion of Rhodesia from its base in
Zambia. As an example of the differing approaches taken by
the two factions throughout the conflict, by mid 1977, Mugabe
had placed 3,000 guerrillas in Rhodesia while Nkomo had
only placed about 200.

The Patriotic Front, then, was only set up to satisfy those at the U.N. and OAU clucking about African unity in the struggle against "white racists," as they called the Smith regime. Militarily, the Patriotic Front was adept only at bayoneting infants, shooting defenseless grandmothers or missionaries and other innocent targets. Their depredations took on sinister connotations: mass murder of workers, cold-blooded murder of missionaries, incidents of cannibalism, large-scale abduction of schoolchildren as a form of terror and guerrilla recruitment, and mining roads to interrupt civilian traffic. These actions seemed designed more to vent the spleen of the Patriotic Front than to win the hearts and minds of the people or, at best, to win hearts and minds not by persuasion, but intimidation. Yet blind supporters in the West overlooked this dark side of the conflict and continued to portray these thugs as "freedom fighters," toasting them in the salons of Washington and New York as liberators, not murderers.

Interestingly enough, it wasn't a black and white situation in Rhodesia. By 1978, 80 percent of the Rhodesian Army was black and all volunteers were black. But that didn't cut any ice with the white, guilt-ridden liberals in the Carter Administration, who, atoning for past sins of white men in the U.S., were determined to soothe their consciences at the expense of whites in Africa. This guilt complex was also felt by mainstream churches. Between 1970 and 1978, some $313,000 was sent to the Soviet and Chinese-backed communists by the World Council of Churches. Some church missions inside Rhodesia were actually used as safe houses by guerrillas. In fact, some so-called men of God were working hand-in-hand with the atheistic Marxists whose hands were dripping with the blood of innocents.

The collapse of Portuguese power in Africa intensified the war in Rhodesia and greatly magnified the problems of the Salisbury government. Soviet-backed communist regimes were in control of Angola and Mozambique. For beleagured Rhodesia, the fall of Mozambique became a strategic nightmare. Overnight, the whole eastern border with Mozambique, almost 700 miles long, suddenly became very vulnerable. Apart from a 125-mile stretch bordering South Africa at

Limpopo River, Rhodesian Security Forces, always short of manpower, now had to guard an enormous 1,800 miles of hostile border. It was an impossible task that would eventually enable the terrorists to pour over the border at will.

Equally important was the fact that the country's import and export lifelines, carrying most of the sanction-busting supplies from the Mozambican ports of Beira and Lourenco Marques (now Maputo), now ran through a country dedicated to the overthrow of the Rhodesian government.

Rhodesia, virtually surrounded by black Botswana, Zambia, Malawi and Mozambique, and isolated from the world community, was totally dependent on the whims of the South African government. Dependence upon South Africa, however, was a two-edged sword. On one hand, South Africa did not relish the idea of a hostile Marxist state on her northern border. It had sent a contingent of police officers to Rhodesia to help the beleagured Rhodesian police force. Fifty helicopters and crew had also been furnished by Pretoria for the counterinsurgency effort. Supplies flowed up two rail lines from South Africa into Rhodesia. Sadly, this aid depended entirely on the good will of the South Africans, which could change at any moment. And change it did, as the result of the machinations of an American diplomat whose policies have proved so disastrous for the West.

Detente, the buzz-word of the early and mid-seventies, was the showcase of the Nixon/Ford/Kissinger foreign policy. It was heady stuff; its infectious nostrums spread south and South African Prime Minister John Vorster decided to play his own regional game.

By the end of 1974, Rhodesian officials estimated that only 70-100 hardcore communist guerrillas remained operating inside Rhodesia. They were on the run, facing total elimination by the Security Forces in a matter of months. Then detente reared its ugly head. As part of Vorster's diplomatic policy to reach out and come to a settlement with black neighboring states, South Africa put the screws on aid passing through their country to Rhodesia. Vorster pressured Smith to try and work out agreements with black nationalists languishing in prison. Under tremendous pressure by Vorster, Smith agreed to a ceasefire and released black political leaders from prison. The pursuit of the few remaining guerrillas was called off and, it was hoped by the advocates of southern African detente, the end of the war was near. Releasing the imprisoned "political" leaders only let them return to the terrorist fold. The eventual victor of the Rhodesian war, Robert Mugabe, was one of those released during the period of detente.

Within days of the ceasefire, the fighting resumed when a group of guerrillas, with a plea to discuss surrender, tricked a group of South African police into an ambush, killing four of them. The ceasefire was a psychological setback for the Salisbury government. A bitter Ian Smith complained rightfully about its effects: "We were on the brink of dealing a knockout blow. We had them on the run; of this there is no doubt. . . . In a sense we dropped our guard and as a result we lost a bit of ground. This not only affected us militarily, but more importantly, psychologically."[1] The guerrilla war resumed.

In 1976, after the highly successful Rhodesian cross-border raid on Mugabe's terrorist training camp at Nyadazonya that killed or injured 1,200 ZANU terrorists, South Africa pulled the rug from under Rhodesia. On August 9, South Africa's Foreign Minister, Dr. Hilgard Muller, stated that he supported the principle of majority rule in Rhodesia. To ensure that Smith got the message, South Africa withdrew 26 of its 40 helicopters on loan to the Rhodesian Air Force and recalled 50 pilots and technicians, cutting the Rhodesians' air strike capacity by half in a single stroke.

Not surprisingly, Henry Kissinger had a hand in the dirty dealing. He promised the South African Prime Minister concessions on American anti-apartheid policies if he persuaded Smith to back down and turn over rule to the blacks. In September, Vorster complied and laid down the law to Smith: Agree to majority rule or South Africa will cut off the supplies. There was to be no going back from this stance, which marked the beginning of the end of white-ruled Rhodesia.

Thankfully, Henry Kissinger was out of a job when Jimmy Carter was elected president. But unfortunately his Africa policy was taken over by a leftist, Marxist sympathizer, U.N. Ambassador Andrew Young. Young and the foreign secretary of the socialist government in England, Dr. David Owen, were pushing for one-man, one-vote rule in Rhodesia that would allow whites in Rhodesia only 10 seats in the 100-seat parliament. Both flew to Salisbury in late 1977 in an attempt to twist Smith's arm and force acceptance of their joint proposal. Smith rejected the Owen-Young giveaway out of hand. The only option left for the Rhodesians was an internal settlement. So Smith began a series of negotiations with the internal black moderate leaders.

On March 3, 1978, history was made when an internal settlement was signed between Ian Smith and three moderate black leaders: Bishop Abel Muzorewa, Rev. Ndabaningi Sithole and Senator Chief Jeremiah Chirau. The tough question of parliamentary representation for all Rhodesians had been resolved, with whites getting 28 seats in the 100-seat parliament. (They had originally sought 34.) The agreement was hailed throughout Rhodesia as a triumph of moderation. A new constitution was drafted, a transitional government was set up, and the first-ever one-man, one-man vote elections would be held at Christmastime and lead to the country's first black prime minister.

After 80 years of white rule, Rhodesia was about to embark upon something inconceivable when UDI was declared—black majority rule. Ian Smith, who declared UDI and vowed there would never be majority rule in his lifetime, had successfully negotiated a compromise that left fellow whites a political minority. It was an extraordinary act of statesmanship that should have made him a giant among world leaders. Just as amazing was the fact that white Rhodesians had given the settlement their blessing.

But alas, recognition was not in store for Rhodesia. The worldwide leftist establishment bitterly attacked the internal settlement. Nkomo and Mugabe denounced the agreement and vowed to continue the war in Rhodesia. The Soviets stepped up their aid to the terrorists and Mugabe's ZANU now began to get huge amounts of it. By mid 1978, the percentage of Soviet military supplies flowing into Mugabe's armories had increased 50 percent.

The internal settlement was supposed to lead to peace. Instead, the war escalated. One of the most brutal acts of the war occurred during this escalatory period. On June 23, 1978, 12 missionaries—eight adults and four children—were raped, hacked and bludgeoned to death at the Elim Pentecostal Mission in eastern Rhodesia by a group of Mugabe's ZANU terrorists. Rhodesian intelligence also picked up plans for an invasion of Rhodesia by Nkomo's ZAPU forces assisted by Cuban surrogates. The man behind this plot was the wily Russian ambassador in Lusaka, Vassily Solodovnikov. Rhodesian Intelligence had grounds for fear. There was evidence of a conventional build up, but according to Moorcraft and McLaughlin in Chimurenga, ". . . the Russians were playing a waiting game and were planning a long-term strategy. The year 1978 was vetoed. When the Cubans suggested a conventional sortie in mid 1979, ZIPRA [the military wing of Nkomo's ZAPU party] rejected the plan even though ZANLA [the military wing of Mugabe's ZANU party] also had made extensive preparations for a conventional incursion. The Russians expected the war to last much longer and were gearing up for a big move in July 1980 or July 1981 depending on military developments. . . ."[2]

Nkomo's guerrillas torpedoed an attempt by Ian Smith to bring him into the internal settlement when they shot down an unarmed, civilian airliner with a surface to air missile. Nkomo removed any chance of being included in the internal settlement when he incensed Rhodesians by chuckling over the shooting during a BBC interview. Ironically, Nkomo and Smith had met in Lusaka to discuss the possibility of bringing Nkomo into the internal agreement just three weeks before the civilian Viscount airliner was shot down.

The Rhodesians struck back by attacking guerrilla bases in Mozambique and Zambia, killing many terrorists and destroying massive amounts of Soviet-supplied equipment. Sadly, their manpower pool was limited, while the guerrillas, through intimidation and indoctrination, could draw on a vast source of manpower. The world was against the Rhodesians. Additionally, they weren't sure the necessary supplies would be available to fight a war. This problem wasn't faced by the guerrillas. As fast as the Rhodesians captured or destroyed their supplies, the Soviets rushed to replace them with larger amounts.

So the war of terror dragged on. The objective was to convince the Rhodesians there would be no peace unless the communists won. It was no longer a question of black majority rule—the whites were totally committed to that concept—the question was twofold: which black group would rule, the moderates or the terrorists, and how would they come to power, by the ballot or bullet. As Nkomo said in August 1978, "I am fighting for power."[3]

The whites were determined that the elections in early 1979 transferring power would be held in spite of the communist attempt to disrupt or cancel them. White voters in Rhodesia held a referendum in January 1979, with 85 percent saying "yes" to the Smith proposal that power would be transferred to the victor in the forthcoming election in April among the black candidates. Shortly afterward, on February 12, 1979, Nkomo's terrorists shot down another civilian Viscount airliner, killing 54 passengers and five crew members, including Rhodesia's first black stewardess. The terrorists had intended to shoot down a plane before the white referendum in the hope that an emotional white backlash would sabotage the Smith plan. In retaliation, the Rhodesian Air Force launched raids into Zambia and bombed one of Nkomo's bases in Angola.

Despite Nkomo's provocation, the Rhodesians were determined to carry out the April elections and organized a 70,000-man security force to protect voters. Never had a ruling minority gone to such trouble to hand over power to a majority. The vaunted threat by communist terrorists to disrupt the elections failed miserably. Only 18 of the 932 polling stations were attacked and none were closed. Sixty-four percent of the electorate voted, giving Abel Muzorewa 51 of the 72 black seats in Parliament. He became the first black African Prime Minister of Rhodesia. What could black terrorists claim they were fighting for now? Black liberation?

The Rhodesians were counting on a promise made by Margaret Thatcher when she was the opposition leader to the socialist Wilson government that as Prime Minister she would recognize the April poll if members of her Conservative Party serving as observers said the election was fair, which they did. But Thatcher reneged on her pledge and sold Rhodesia out to the Marxists under threats by Nigeria to cut off oil supplies to Britain if the government recognized the new Zimbabwe. This, coupled with threats that the British Commonwealth might actually break up over the Rhodesian issue, gave ammunition to left-leaning members of the British foreign service to force the sell-out on Thatcher.

The British were assisted by fellow-travelers in the Carter Administration and American "observers" such as Congressman Stephen Solarz, (D-NY) who helped shape the policy that Muzorewa's government and the internal settlement be dismantled.

As could be expected, the Soviets also got in the act. They stepped up arms deliveries to the terrorists after the April elections to reinforce and make self-fulfilling the prophecy of Western liberal apologists that recognition would be countered by intensified war. The obvious solution was to get rid of Muzorewa and stage new elections under the auspices of the British. The problem was how to persuade Muzorewa to step down. The critical task, according to Dr. Richard T. McCormack, a former Assistant Secretary of State for Economic and Business Affairs, "was to convince each involved party that they stood to gain by new elections and a new constitution."

So the following assurances were made by the British: The Thatcher government told General Peter Walls, head of the Rhodesian Armed Forces, that Britain would never permit the Marxist Mugabe to come to power; it told white Rhodesians that their interests would be protected; it told Muzorewa that the British objective was to give him more power, to free him from excessive white influence, and enable him to be the dominant factor in his nation. With these promises, the parties agreed to a new election in Zimbabwe.

Arm-twisting by their hosts in Zambia and Mozambique forced the terrorists to accept the proposal as a new opportunity for them, which indeed it was. Their morale was low— Muzorewa's election and the strong positive response by large segments of American and European opinion had discouraged them. Vigorous action by Rhodesian Security Forces had inflicted high casualty rates that were causing concern in high guerrilla councils. Thus, they agreed that there were good reasons to seek a less painful route to power. So the British got everyone to the conference table on September 10, 1979, and the infamous Lancaster House Conference was underway. It dragged on until Christmas, with all sides trying to got the best possible deal. Since British intelligence had bugged the conference, Britain knew just how far each side could be pushed.

The British plan, in essence, was to create a coalition government headed by Nkomo that contained both the whites and Muzorewa. Under this plan, Mugabe was to be cut out; any involvement on Mugabe's part with the envisioned government would be in a subordinate role in the new cabinet. British pressure on Samora Machel, the dictator of communist Mozambique, forced him to tell Mugabe that if he refused to cooperate and resumed the war, Mozambique would boot his forces out of the country. Without Mozambique as a sanctuary, Mugabe's ZANU would collapse, so he reluctantly agreed.

On December 21, 1979, all parties to the conference signed the final agreement, with a ceasefire and fragile peace to follow on December 28.

It was a masterful job of convincing everyone they would get a piece of the cake: Nkomo felt he was the consensus choice for prime minister; Muzorewa believed the British government wanted to increase his power; the whites believed the British would guarantee their safety in the new Nkomo coalition; Mugabe thought his terrorist network and strong Shona tribal base inside Rhodesia would serve him well. This was diplomacy at its shameful best.

So the eighties dawned on a changing Rhodesia preparing for its second election to choose new rulers, which was scheduled for April. The only fear of the British was that Muzorewa would duplicate his smash electoral success of a year before and make the task of persuading him to take a back seat to Nkomo even more difficult. They hoped that since Mugabe and Muzorewa were from the same tribal base, Mugabe would cut into the Shona vote and reduce Muzorewa's vote, making it easier to see that he took second place in the new government.

A potential danger existed in this scheme: Everyone

involved knew that Mugabe would do very well in the elections if he were able to use his terrorist network to intimidate the voters in the Shona Tribal Trust Lands. The British assured one and all that they would strictly police the elections and disqualify Mugabe if he attempted to intimidate voters. It was a shallow promise, since Mugabe killed, maimed and terrorized his competition out of the Shona tribal areas and the British didn't lift a finger to stop it. In concert with Mugabe's campaign of intimidation was his main campaign theme—that he had brought the war and only he could end it. Otherwise, it was back to the bush and more killing.

The people of Rhodesia had been killing each other for 15 years and were tired of the war. They were in a frame of mind in which they'd have voted for anyone if he offered an end to the conflict. The war-weary Rhodesians, especially blacks, weren't interested in fancy theories of politics and government—they were worried about physical survival. And by turning their back on Mugabe's intimidation tactics, the British tacitly condoned them, paving the road to his ascendency.

Since assuming power, Mugabe's regime has been a typical bloody, socialist disaster. Zimbabwe is a land of misery, oppression and bloodshed—a far cry from what its liberators had promised.

1. Paul Moorcraft and Peter McLaughlin, *Chimurenga: The War in Rhodesia 1965-1980*. (Cape Town, South Africa: Sygma Books, 1982), p. 31.

2. Ibid.

3. Paul Moorcraft, *Contact II*. (Johannesburg, South Africa: Sygma, 1981), p. 58.

The author with troops of 101 Battalion (SWATF) on an operation against SWAPO terrorists

8

The Coup That Wasn't

The British had concocted the Lancaster House Settlement with the view of installing Nkomo as the head of the new black government. Abel Muzorewa was to be the vice-president, Mugabe, the odd man out. General Wall was assured by the British that they would never permit Mugabe to come to power. They claimed they were just as repelled by his philosophy and ruthless methods of operation as were white Rhodesians. But the Rhodesians, with the behind-the-scenes knowledge of and encouragement by the British, made a contingency plan in case Mugabe confounded the experts and won.

The British thought Muzorewa and Mugabe would split the Shona tribal vote and that Nkomo would capture the Metebele and white votes. Unfortunately, they didn't count on Mugabe's terrorist network in the Shona tribal lands and his murderous intimidation tactics that drew thousands of votes from Muzorewa.

Shortly after all parties had signed the Lancaster House Agreement, a meeting was held in Salisbury at the air force cricket pavillion of the Rhodesian Security Force unit commanders. Senior officers said that Mugabe could not and would not win the upcoming elections. It was made perfectly clear to the unit commanders that, if necessary, military force would be used to prevent an unexpected Mugabe victory. As a result of this meeting, a special operating committee made up of high-ranking army, air force and intelligence officials was established to plan for a military response should their worst fear, a Mugabe victory, be realized.

They came up with a two-pronged operation: phase one was called Operation Hectic and involved covert action against selected Mugabe terrorist leaders; the second phase, Operation Quartz, was to eliminate major Mugabe headquarter elements in Salisbury and other targets, primarily the assembly areas of Mugabe's ZANLA terrorists who were scattered throughout the countryside.

Operation Hectic was targeted at the leadership of ZANLA and supposed to eliminate it. Its objective was to kill Mugabe, Simon Muzendo, vice-president of ZANLA, and Rex Nhongo, ZANLA's senior military commander. If Hectic failed, so would Quartz because the leaders could scurry back to the bush and resume their terrorist war.

Operation Quartz was based on the fact that thousands of ZANLA and ZIPRA terrorists (or former terrorists since they were now inside Rhodesia to vote in the forthcoming elections) were massed in known assembly points inside the country. Kept apart so they wouldn't start fighting one another, both groups were to be bombed and strafed by the air force, which would be guided to respective targets by Security Force personnel who were secretly watching the areas from their hidden observation positions. These operations were only to be used if Mugabe won the election and, more importantly, if the combined Operations Headquarters of the Rhodesian Army specifically ordered it, by means of a special code word. If Hectic and Quartz were given the go-ahead, Joshua Nkomo would be named the new head of Zimbabwe.

The critical task of Hectic, the elimination of the ZANLA leadership, was entrusted to the elite Rhodesian Special Air Service (SAS) Regiment under the command of Lt. Col. Gareth Barret. One squadron of the regiment was to kill Mugabe at his home in Salisbury and another was to kill ZANLA vice president Muzenda as well as about 100 ZANLA men billeted in a local Medical Arts Centre that was serving as temporary headquarters. A third squadron was to attack the temporary military headquarters of the Patriotic Front, the loose alliance of ZANLA and ZIPRA. This target, the University of Rhodesia's Audio-Visual Centre, was the only one that housed both ZANLA and ZIPRA.

The plan called for the building to be surrounded. Word would be slipped to Nkomo's ZIPRA supporters that the building was to be attacked, giving them the opportunity to surrender. Those desiring to surrender would be allowed to make their way out of the building and into a holding area. Those declining the offer would be killed. Since this target was military headquarters, it was expected that the terrorists would be heavily armed and would put up a fight. The commander of the squadron, Captain Mike Reid, ordered extra firepower to give his troops the decided edge. Eight captured Soviet-supplied T-55 tanks with 100mm guns, a 12.7mm heavy machine gun, and a 7.62 coaxial mounted machine gun would surround and blast away at the building. Also, Captain Reid's forces had a 20mm cannon, RPG-7 rocket launchers, and automatic rifles. When the tanks and other assorted power were finished, the squadron would storm what was left of the building and kill any survivors. No quarter would be given.

Hectic required only routine reconnaissance. SAS men were able to walk freely through the city every day in civilian clothes or disguised as Police Reservists ostensibly checking access routes, guard posts, etc. The information gathered on the targets was extremely detailed. For example, in the case of the three-story university building and the Medical Arts Centre, the SAS had complete sets of plans. Reid's soldiers also knew who slept in what bed, what weapons each individual used and where weapons such as RPG-7 rocket launchers and machine guns were kept. They were also able to drive around the city in convoys on their way to drop off troops who were manning strategic points in the city. The residents of Salisbury were familiar with heavily armed troops driving around the city in trucks and armored cars.

An official rumor was circulated that SAS men were also cruising around the city in plain sight as a morale booster for the whites. While true, this also gave the SAS fantastic cover to be constantly driving past their intended targets to update their intelligence and work out their timing without arousing the suspicions of the enemy. By being on the streets in their vehicles, the SAS could be at their assigned targets in minutes after getting the go-ahead to launch Operation Hectic.

Hectic was one of the most detailed, well-planned operations the SAS had undertaken during the war: Everything from starting fires, then smothering them, to handling casualties and setting up communications was rehearsed over and over; the plan and timing had been honed to perfection; the rehearsals had exceeded everyone's expectations and the back-up firepower was the best SAS could offer. When the planning and training were finally over, the SAS troops knew what they had to do and how they had to do it. The observation posts overlooking assembly areas were manned; they were ready to call in jets on the targets; planes were fueled and their bomb racks loaded; all crews were on standby, waiting for the code word that would begin the operation.

On Tuesday, March 4, when the results of the election were to be announced at 9 a.m., the SAS was in position at strategic intersections in Salisbury, just minutes away from the targets. As the clock crept closer to 9 o'clock, the tension increasing with each slowly-passing, unnerving second, it began to look as if the code word wouldn't be coming, The SAS men thought Mugabe had lost the election and the operations weren't needed. Sadly, they were wrong. SAS men switched their radios from the military frequency to the local station and heard the astounding news: Mugabe had not only won, but had crushed his opponents at the polls.

The reaction of the SAS, once the initial shock of the news wore off, was one of immense disgust. They had been had. All the effort, planning, reconnaissance, rehearsal and expectations were a waste of time. How many times had they had Mugabe in their sights during the pre-election period, but couldn't fire the fatal round. Now he was Prime Minister of Zimbabwe.

What had happened? A plausible theory had it that Nkomo, the beneficiary of the plan, was briefed on it and rejected it, saying he could not be seen taking the country from white officers. How could he sell such an event to the West? One could only imagine the howls of indignation that would have been raised by the Carter Administration if the coup had taken place.

Or perhaps the existence of a top-level spy in the Rhodesia Combined Operations had tipped Mugabe off. There was such a mole at the upper level of Rhodesian intelligence, comparable in rank to a deputy director of the CIA, who could have warned Mugabe. According to documents seen by the author and testimony by a former Rhodesian police officer in charge of the anti-terrorist police squad, the individual in question was a spy. Interestingly enough, he retained the same job in Mugabe's government as he had had in Ian Smith's. If Mugabe had been informed of the plot by a spy, the only way to escape was to avoid the target building on the morning election results were announced—which he did.

Even after the election, many still thought a coup could work. Some worked frantically to come up with a new plan, but their efforts came to naught. General Walls is reported to have said that with the number of Mugabe's terrorists in the country, a coup attempt would last only 48 hours. Undoubtedly, such a move would have restarted the civil war.

Perhaps the best explanation of why there was no coup was that none was ever intended to take place. A member of the Combined Operations planning team said that although the possibility of a coup was discussed, the idea was quickly dropped, for the wrath and abuse of the world would descend on Rhodesia's head like a guillotine if one had been tried. "We discussed it for 15 minutes,"[1] the planning team member said. Perhaps in the final analysis, the coup was nothing more than an exercise to keep the Rhodesian security forces busy and out of mischief during this critical period in the country's history.

1. Barbara Cole, *The Elite, The Story of the Rhodesian Special Air Service.* (Transkei: Three Knights, 1984), p. 420.

9

Trouble In Mugabe's Paradise

Robert Mugabe came to power in 1980 using Marxist tactics of terror and intimidation. One example of his methods will give you the flavor of Mugabe's political campaign style. Prior to the 1980 elections, when the ceasefire went into effect, Mugabe's and Nkomo's forces were put into designated assembly points where they could be kept from each other's throats yet allowed to participate in the election. Mugabe's high command deliberately kept out a large number of his combatants who were replaced in the assembly with young people called the "mujubus." His trained guerrillas cached their arms and moved among the locals in Tribal Trust Lands, issuing threats describing the horrors that would befall them if they failed to vote for Mugabe. The British, who were supervising the 1980 elections, knew of such intimidation tactics, but brushed them aside, preferring instead to rid themselves of the Rhodesian problem as quickly as possible.

In short, Mugabe terrorized his way into power.

The same or an even greater level of intimidation occurred in the campaign prior to the 1985 elections. Dire threats were made to countless voters that they had better vote for Mugabe's party or else. To drive the point home, certain individuals were selected and branded as "sell-outs," then murdered or tortured to serve as examples of the fate of those who voted the wrong way.

Mugabe made excuses for delaying the election date from March to July in the 1985 elections. Another of his malicious and vindictive tricks was the reduction of time to nominate candidates from two weeks to five days, putting opposition parties under severe strain to get candidates prepared in time for the election.

In short, the elections were corrupt from beginning to end. In many polling places, the final figures exceeded the tally of registered voters by ridiculous margins. In some 18 instances, the votes exceeded the number of registered voters by 5,000 or more. In Sabrina, the constituency of Mugabe's parliamentary seat, the votes exceeded registration lists by more than 20,000, or 60 percent. Since Mugabe controls the press, it was mobilized to give his ruling party shamelessly favorable coverage and support. All ZANU meetings and rallys were extensively advertised and covered by the government-controlled media, while the opposition was given short shrift. In fact, its leaders were often denigrated or belittled. And the terror, beatings and intimidation continued.

In 1983, Mugabe told the 6th Brigade, an all-Shona paramilitary unit trained by North Koreans, that the rate at which the people accepted Marxism would depend on the "persuasion" that they, the soldiers, brought to bear. The infamous 5th Brigade, also all Shona and North Korean-trained, was specifically deployed in Matabeleland to "persuade" the Ndebele tribesmen who are loyal supporters of Mugabe's opponent—Joshua Nkomo—to support their tribal enemy Mugabe.

The 5th Brigade's campaign of murder, torture and harassment served notice on all Zimbabweans of what to expect if they dared oppose Mugabe's ruling party. So vicious were the 5th Brigade's atrocities that they gave rise to the unit's name, "Gukuranhundi," meaning "the cloudburst that sweeps all away in its path."

Mugabe's heavyhanded tactics didn't stop after he "won" the 1985 "election." Joshua Nkomo and other opposition figures have been subjected to a vicious campaign of terror. After the elections, ZANU's Youth Brigade and Women's League launched a six-day orgy of violence, running amok, burning, stoning and murdering those even suspected of membership in opposition parties. More than 700 hundred homes were destroyed and numerous people, including two opposition party candidates, were murdered during the melee.

Amnesty International, the liberal, London-based human rights organization, reported a sharp increase in arrests and torture of suspected government opponents in Zimbabwe in 1985, including beatings and electric shocks at detention camps. At least 150 people were arrested and held in Bulawayo. Citing accounts from a wide variety of sources, Amnesty said detainees were hung upside down and beaten while their heads were submerged in buckets of water. Others' heads were placed in canvas bags full of water and they were left to lose consciousness or drown.

Mugabe's imposition of totalitarian, Marxist-Leninist rule, aimed at creating a one-party state, is breeding a resistance movement amongst the Ndebele, the tribal base of most of his political opponents.

The Ndebele are an offshoot of the Zulu tribe in South Africa. In the early part of the 19th century, under a leader named Mzilikazi, they broke away from the parent tribe and trekked northward to establish a kingdom in an area known as Matabeleland in present-day Zimbabwe.

They were a proud, war-like people who looked down with contempt on the indigenous members of various Shona tribes who inhabited the area northeast of their new domain. The Ndebele conducted frequent raids into Shona terrritory, extracting tribute in the form of cattle and women. In general, the Shona were regarded as vassals of the Ndebele kingdom. This situation lasted until white settlers arrived in Rhodesia in 1890 and imposed a peaceful co-existence on the warring tribes.

Nevertheless, the historic rivalry and animosity among the tribes persists today and fuels Mugabe's violence against his political opponents, the strongest of whom also happen to be his tribe's ancient enemy, the Ndebele.

The initial black nationalist movement formed in Rhodesia, however, did have a national flavor—its membership included representatives from almost all tribal communities. The man regarded as the figurehead and "father of black nationalism" was a Ndebele pro-Soviet communist named Joshua Nkomo. However, the traditional mistrust and rivalry between the two major groups split black nationalist ranks in the early sixties. With rare exceptions, the different political parties that were formed subsequently divided along tribal lines. Major, bloody clashes between rival parties in the battle for membership and dominance were the result, with a succession of parties being banned and their leaders detained by Rhodesian authorities.

In the struggle for power in Rhodesia, the terrorist forces were again divided by tribal loyalties. ZIPRA, based in Zambia and supported by the Soviet Union, is a Ndebele fighting unit under the political banner of ZAPU. ZANLA is a Shona force under the political wing of ZANU which operated from Tanzania and, after the Lisbon coup, from Mozambique. It was backed by Red China, North Korea and Yugoslavia. There were many clashes between the rival forces at shared terrorist training camps and during incursions into Rhodesian territory.

Eventually, under pressure from leaders of neighboring, so-called Black Confrontational States, the two forces joined in a fragile alliance called the Patriotic Front (PF). It was a very uneasy and short-lived union that papered over huge cracks between the two groups.

The 1980 elections in Zimbabwe arrived and the shaky alliance came apart. It was originally anticipated that the common roll election, held in terms of the Lancaster House Agreement, would be contested by the PF as a unified political organization. That illusion was shattered by ZANU's Robert Mugabe as he sought political dominance for his Shona people. Nkomo and his political movement retained the title PF or PF(ZAPU).

The election campaign was marked by bitter feuding and intimidation. The main instigators and perpetrators of intimidation were ex-ZANLA combatants who roamed the marginal areas and stopped other parties from campaigning. Votes were cast along tribal lines with the results reflecting areas of influence. The PF swept the board in Matebeland and secured some seats in the Midlands. ZANU (PF) captured the vast majority of seats in traditional Shona habitats.

After assuming the reins of power, Mugabe, as the majority leader of the government, embarked on a so-called policy of reconciliation; introduced purely for tactical reasons and to buy time with which Mugabe and his gang of thugs could consolidate power. ZAPU leader Joshua Nkomo and some of his senior lieutenants were invited to join the government. The three fighting forces—ZANLA, ZIPRA and the former Rhodesian Security Forces—were progressively integrated into a new national army. This period of reconciliation didn't last long. A major battle between government forces and ZIPRA units took place on the outskirts of Bulawayo. But for the discipline and military efficiency of the ex-Rhodesian element in the government contingent, the Ndebele, then and there, might have established a semi-autonomous state. Using this conflict and the alleged discovery of ZIPRA arms caches as excuses, Mugabe purged Nkomo and his senior aides from his cabinet and launched his campaign of terror and intimidation against ZAPU. The late former ZIPRA Commander, Lookout Musaka, and its intelligence chief, Dumiso Dabengwa, were detained and charged with treason. They were acquitted in court, but were promptly redetained. Musaka died in prison and Dabengwa was only released a short time ago after agreeing to stay out of Zimbabwean politics. Obviously, Mugabe's opponents cannot expect relief from a jury.

This launched the current Ndebele resistance movement. Denied relief by the ballot box and the jury box, the Ndebele sought relief from the cartridge box. Angered by the insults to their leaders, a number of ex-ZIPRA members took to the bush once again and began a violent campaign against government institutions, officials and supporters in the Matabele Provinces. These groups were labeled as dissidents and are still a thorn in the side of the Mugabe regime, which is reacting in typical Marxist fashion. Rather than resolve the Ndebele grievance through negotiations, the regime embarked on a brutal campaign of repression against the Ndebele nation.

Mugabe formed two all-Shona army political brigades, the North Korean-trained 5th and 6th, whose sole allegiance is to the ruling party. Countless innocent civilians have been murdered, tortured and mutilated by this political army. The government withheld relief supplies for the Matabele Provinces in an effort to starve the inhabitants into submission.

But these tactics have failed to subdue the Ndebele

nation. Mugabe and his thugs have repeated, and their Party Congresses have confirmed, that they intend to turn Zimbabwe into a one-party Marxist state. In concert with these actions, Mugabe is trying to woo Nkomo and some of his officials, to persuade them to disband ZAPU and merge with ZANU. Nkomo is in a no-win situation. If he joins Mugabe, he forfeits his leadership of the Ndebele to young turks prepared to continue the struggle against Shona domination. He can refuse to join Mugabe and continue to be the titular head of the Ndebeles. In either case Mugabe will contine his persecution of Matabeland. At present, a substantial portion of Zimbabwe's army is deployed in Matabele province where they continue to terrorize and intimidate the locals. Despite these facts, Ndebele resistance to Shona domination continues unabated. The number of resistance fighters in the field is uncertain, but they remain an active force.

If Mugabe's demand of a political merger with Nkomo is forced through by bribery, coercion or both, the ranks of the resistance will swell still further. Thus far, the resistance has lacked a strong leader, since most of the competent candidates are held in Mugabe's dungeons. It is highly probable that the situation will deteriorate in Zimbabwe until a wide-spread revolt erupts, leading to an independent Ndebele nation. It would be in the interest of South Africa for this to happen, since a separate, independent Ndebele state would be far more concerned with its survival than the crusade to liberate blacks in South Africa.

Zimbabwe had a relatively well-developed, industrial infrastructure—the best in the region outside South Africa's. However, it is deteriorating under Mugabe's socialist policies. By virtue of the existence of that infrastructure, it is the only country through which a conventional attack on the Republic of South Africa is feasible. Both the South Africans and Soviets are aware of this fact. The Balkanization of Zimbabwe would reduce this danger for South Africa. As events unfold in both Zimbabwe and South Africa, namely, more ANC mine incidents along the border and a continuation of terror against the Ndebele, South African support for the

Ndebele resistance movement is not beyond the realm of possiblity and would be a serious policy alternative for the South Africans.

The long-standing, bitter dispute between the Shona and the Ndebele will not disappear overnight. Until those differences are settled, they will continue to be a thorn in the side of Robert Mugabe as he imposes totalitarian control on Zimbabwe.

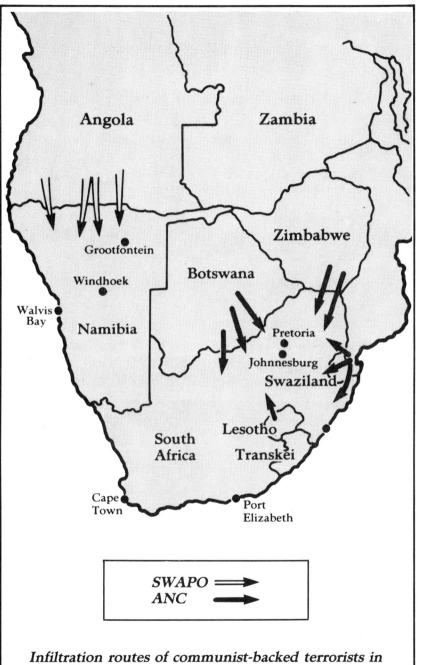

SWAPO ⟹
ANC ━━▶

Infiltration routes of communist-backed terrorists in southern Africa.

SWAPO's war of terror is directed against the unarmed civilian population. A SWAPO bomb wrecks a medical clinic in Ovamboland, SWA/Namibia.

The SWAPO terrorist war causes destruction to the civilian population in both Angola and SWA/Namibia.

SWAPO landmines destroy civilian vehicles.

The United Nations supports terrorism. Food supplies found in a captured SWAPO terrorist base. Note on the label: UNHCR stands for United Nations High Commissioner for Refugees.

10
African National Congress: The Soviets' Tool In South Africa

The destabilization of the Republic of South Africa is being carried out by a Soviet-backed terror group called the African National Congress (ANC). Its activities are tightly controlled by the outlawed South African Communist Party, which receives marching orders from the Soviet Union.

The South African Communist Party, founded on July 20, 1921, is one of the oldest communist parties outside the Soviet Union and is totally loyal and subservient to the Kremlin. In its early years, the communist movement in South Africa was aimed solely at whites. It chauvinistically assumed that only the white working class had revolutionary potential; that the black population was pastoral, outside the class conflict of the capitalist world—irrelevant to the revolution. Even today, the South African Communist Party is very sensitive about this issue.

However, after the 1922 mineworkers' strike caused by post World War I economic woes in South Africa, the communists began recruiting blacks. This was the beginning of the slow infiltration and takeover of the black nationalist movement in South Africa. In 1926, James Gomede, a member of the South African Communist Party, was elected President General of the ANC, marking the first communist infiltration in the ANC leadership. It wouldn't be the last.

The ANC, founded in 1912 by a number of black lawyers, was to pressure the government for an integrated South Afican society. its original name was the South African Native National Congress. In 1925, the group changed its name to the South African National Congress, but for financial and administrative reasons, it remained moribund until the Second World War.

In 1943, the ANC adopted a new constitution allowing the admission of non-blacks for the first time. A year later, a Youth League was formed which became noted for its militant advocacy of black supremacy and goals that were "to arouse and encourage national consciousness and unity among African youth and to assist, support and reinforce the African national people. . . ."¹ The League intensified its militant action against South African race laws by organizing demonstrations and protest marches in the early 1960's. All the while, Youth League activities were changing the ANC. Dr. A.B. Xuma was forced to step down as head of the ANC in 1949 under Youth League pressure. He was succeeded by J.S. Maroka, who quickly found he couldn't get along with the Youth League either, and was replaced by Albert Luthuli.

In 1955, Luthuli's ANC collaborated with the Trade Union Federation, a communist front, and the radical Congress of Democrats and participated in a conference organized by the Congress of the People. The objective of the Congress, an ad hoc body set up by a wing of the South African Communist Party, was to rubber-stamp approve of the so-called Freedom Charter, the brainchild of the South African Communist Party. The Freedom Charter was the ANC's "Front" to disguise its push for Marxist-Leninist socialism in order to retain Western and liberal support for its terrorist campaign inside South Africa.

The ANC accepted the Freedom Charter, but three years later a rift developed in the ANC's ranks. Some members wished to keep the ANC an all-black organization. Other members didn't want to cooperate with the SACP. Unable to reconcile their differences, a splinter group formed and split from the ANC under the leadership of Robert Sobukwe. It was called the Pan Africanist Congress (PAC).

Friction between the two groups, which developed as both actively sought the support of blacks, caused each to adopt increasingly radical positions. The competitive radicalism between the two led to the bloody Sharpeville and Cato Manor incidents in 1960, after which both organizations were banned under the South African Suppression of Communism Act of April 1960. This ban severely restricted the activities of

Luthuli, who was personally subjected to the ban, and a change of leadership was made in the ANC: Nelson Mandela, a self-professed communist, took the reins of power from Luthuli. (Under Mandela's leadership the ANC adopted violence to achieve its goals. Mandela's terrorist activities led to his arrest, conviction and life sentence in Pollsmoor Prison. He is a cause celebre of everyone on the left from Ted Kennedy to Mikhail Gorbachev.)

On December 16, 1961, the ANC established a military wing, Umkhonto We Sizwe ("Spear of the Nation"), that began a campaign of murder and terror to overthrow the South African government. In 1969, the ANC held a conference in Tanzania and adopted resolutions directing a war of terror against the South African people. The ANC decided to intensify the armed struggle, to involve working class youths, Asians and coloreds and form alliances with Marxist movements such as ZAPU (in Rhodesia), FRELIMO (in Mozambique), SWAPO (in Namibia) and the MPLA (in Angola).

Not all participants at the conference were happy that the ANC was jumping into bed with the Marxists. Roland Stranbridge noted: ". . . This decision, which is still effective, caused serious divisions within the organization. These came to a head in 1975, when ANC leader Ambrose Makiwane charged that 'the trouble the African people have at present is that our strategy and tactics are in the hands of, and dominated by, a small clique of non-Africans.' He blamed this on 'the disastrous Morogoro Consultative Conference [the 1969 Tanzanian meeting] which opened ANC membership to non-Africans.' Makiwane and seven others were expelled from the ANC leadership in an executive memorandum released in London on December 11, 1975. They complained that there was an absence of democratic consultation within the organization, that the traditional ANC policies and ideology had been diluted, and that the SACP, whose leaders were white, had effective control of the ANC."[2] *The African Communist,* a publication of SACP, spells out the relationship of the SACP and ANC very clearly: "Today, the ANC and SACP are embraced in the common front for liberation."[3]

Proof of the ANC's complete dominance by the South

African Communist Party is the presence of well-known SACP members in the command structure of the ANC. Dr. Yusuf Dadoo, chairman of the SACP, is chairman of the ANC National Executive Committee and a member of the ANC Revolutionary Council; Moses Mabhida, chief political commissar of the ANC, is Secretary-General of the SACP; Joe Slovo, member of the SACP, is a member of the ANC National Executive Committee, a member of the ANC Revolutionary Council and head of Spear of the Nation, military wing of the ANC.

Although the ANC has bases in non-communist countries such as Zambia, most are in communist nations such as Angola and Mozambque. The ANC is closely allied with the radical Marxist Polisario Front as well as the PLO. The ANC has, on countless occasions, cooperated with the Soviets or their proxies and has no qualms about bragging to the world of this relationship. ANC's monthly magazane, *Sechaba*, reporting in its September 1984 issue on an ANC delegation in Nicaragua to celebrate the fifth anniversary of the Sandinista communist revolution, said, "Like the Cuban revolution, the revolution in Nicaragua is under attack from the United States and its allies. . . . The solidarity of the ANC with Nicaragua . . . expresses the fact that the same struggle is common to both."[4]

The ANC also hates Israel and loves the PLO with equal passion. According to *Sechaba*: "The African National Congress has, on numerous occasions and in various international fora, declared that the voice of the Palestinian poeple can only be represented by its authentic organization and leadership, the Palestine Liberation Organization, which represents the aspirations of the Palestinian people."[5] (1983)

Commenting on U.S. policy in the Middle East, ANC President Oliver Tambo, mouthing the pro-Soviet PLO party line, said, "During the past year, this regime was encouraged in its counter-offensive by the criminal activities of Zionist Israel against the people of Lebanon and Palestinian refugees in that country and the Palestine Liberation Organization, the PLO. After repeated raids, aggression into Lebanon, during the course of which the Zionist Israeli troops mercilessly butchered both Lebanese and Palestinians and sought to

destroy whole cities, the Zionists ultimately occupied virtually the whole of Beirut and other parts of Lebanon."[6]
     The ANC parrots official Soviet ideological publications,
using rhetoric that could have been penned by the staff of
Pravda. Again, quoting *Sachaba*: "We too must speak out
against attempts of the United States to impose its will on the
peoples of the world. This policy has already resulted in the
criminal invasion of Grenada, the undeclared war against
Nicaragua and the direct intervention of the United States in
El Salvador, in support of a gang of murderers. It has led to a
reign of terror against the people of Palestine and their
organization, the PLO, as well as the people of Lebanon. It
has helped Morocco to ignore the resolutions of the OAU and
to maintain its colonial hold over the people of the Western
Sahara."[7]
     In his statement to the U.N. General Assembly in Novem-
ber 1982 Tambo said, "We cannot close, Mr. President,
without addressing a special word of support to SWAPO and
the people of Namibia, the PLO and the Palestinian people,
the Polisario Front and the people of Sakroui Arab Democratic Republic, to the Farabundo Marti National Liberation
Front and the people of El Salvador and the FRETILIN and
the people of West Timor, as well as all other people struggling
for their national liberation. We affirm our solidarity with the
Frontline and other independent states in southern Africa."[8]
     The Soviet Union readily admitted its support of the ANC
in an article published in the December 1982 Soviet journal
World Marxist Review: "The national liberation movement in
SA largely owes its present scope and clarity of perspectives
to our party's tireless activity in the organizational, political
and ideological sphere. The well-thought-out and clear-cut
concepts and tenets based on the theory of scientific socialism
are no longer the exclusive assets of communists, but have
been variously spread to broad sections of the fighters for
liberation. . . . We are the party of fighters and activists
working in the very midst of the masses. The communist
leaders and rank-and-file members have initiated, organized
and taken part in all the battles against racist oppressors. We
were also a party to the decision to go over to the armed
struggle. There are many communists among the Umkhonto

we Sizwe combat units, including their commanders. . . . South African revolutionaries deeply appreciate the all-round assistance rendered them by Socialist countries, headed by the Soviet Union."[9]

The terrorists of the ANC also receive aid and help from the international communist terror network. For example, a member of the French Communist party is the main suspect in an attack on the nuclear power plant in Koeberg, near Cape Town, in December 1982. The late Henri Curiel, of the French-based organization Solidarite, gave logistical support to Soviet-backed terrorist movements such as the Red Army Faction in Germany, the Red Brigades in Italy, as well as the South African Okhela (Spark) group, which is linked to the ANC.

Interestingly enough, after the ANC was forced out of Mozambique, it beefed up operations in Botswana, creating a whole new set of problems for South Africa. As a result, there has been an unusual increase in activity at the Soviet Embassy in Gaberone. French intelligence has warned that this embassy is the KFB's headquarters for operations in South Africa. Manpower levels there are far larger than those required to handle routine affairs in Botswana. In fact, the embassy monitors all South African diplomatic, military and police radio traffic.

The Soviet Ambassador to Botswana, Nicolai Petrov, is believed to be a general in the KGB. He is an agent-provocateur of some note, having previously been expelled from three African countries: Kenya in 1967, Ghana in 1971, and Mali in 1978. Operations elsewhere in black Africa, particularly in Zaire, the Congo, the Central African Federation and Cameroon are believed to be coordinated from the KGB Embassy in Luanda. Much of the intelligence acquired by KGB officers in Gaberone and Luanda is passed to the Institute of African Affairs in Moscow headed by Anatole Gromyko, son of Soviet President and former Foreign Minister Andrei Gromyko.

Not surprisingly, most weapons used by the ANC are of Soviet or East German origin. ANC cadres are trained by Eastern block instructors or at terrorist schools in either the Soviet Union or Eastern bloc countries. In testimony before

Senator Jeremiah Denton's (R-AL) Subcommittee on Terrorism and Security, a former ANC member spoke about Soviet control of the ANC. The witness, Bartholomew Hlapane, a former member of the Central Committee of the SACP and a member of the National Executive Committee of the ANC, told the subcommittee: "... No major decision could be taken by the ANC without the concurrence and approval of the Central Committe of the SACP. Most major developments were, in fact, initiated by the Central Committee."[10]

Plans used by the ANC are coordinated in Moscow and passed to the SACP which in turn passes them to the ANC. Hlapane also said that "the military wing of the ANC, also known as Umkhonro we Sizwe, was the brainchild of the SACP, and after the decision to create it had been taken, Joe Slovo and J.B. Marks were sent by the Central Committee of the SACP to Moscow to organize arms and ammunition and to raise funds for Umkhonto We Sizwe."[11] Slovo, of Lithuanian descent and reputed to be a colonel in the KGB, is officially designated as "Deputy Chief" of Umkhonto We Sizwe and is still a member of the National Executive Committee of the ANC and of the Central Committee of the SACP. After years of residence in London, following his departure from South Africa in 1963, he returned to southern Africa in 1975 after FRELIMO's accession to power in Mozambique.

Hlapane also testifed that the sole source of funds for Umkhonto We Sizwe during the period that he acted as Treasurer of the SACP was the Communist Party itself. In revenge for his testimony, Hlapane was murdered in his home in Sewoto, December 16, 1982 by an ANC assassin armed with a Soviet-made, AK-47 assault rifle.

Senator Denton concluded: "... we found incontrovertible evidence of Soviet penetration and control of the two major terrorist organizations in the region, the African National Congress (ANC) and the South West Africa People's Organization (SWAPO). A chilling tale of Soviet manipulation emerged from the testimony of former members of the organizations and the documents included in the record."[12]

Despite this, the U.S. State Department, the media, and academia remain unconvinced that the ANC is a Soviet-controlled terror group. In fact, the group is nothing more than an integrated organ of Soviet foreign policy that is being used to destabilize South Africa.

1. Contemporary African Political Organizations, Roland Stanbridge quoted in reprint of the Chairman of the Subcommittee on Security and Terrorism, Nov. 1982, p. 5.

2. Roland Stanbridge, *Contemporary African Political Organizations and Movements.* Quoted in the report of the chairman of the Subcommittee on Security and Terrorism (November 1982), p. 7.

3. Sol Dubula, "The Two Pillars of Our Struggle: Reflections on the Relationship Between the ANC and SACP," *The African Communist,* No. 87 (Jan. 1981), p. 30.

4. "ANC Delegation Visits Nicaragua," *Sechaba* (official organ of the African National Congress of South Africa) (September 1984), p. 24.

5. "Zionism and Apartheid Wedded Ideologies," *Sechaba* (February 1983), p. 25.

6. Speech of O.R. Tambo, given January 8, 1983, reported in *Sechaba* (March 1983), p. 4.

7. "President's Message for 1984," *Sechaba* (March 1984), p. 11.

8. Statement of Oliver Tambo to the United Nations General Assembly on November 9, 1982.

9. The Aida Parker Newsletter, Special ANC Issue, Vol. 71 (1985), p. 3.

10. Report of the Chairman of the Subcommittee on Security and Terrorism (November 1982), p. 21.

11. Ibid.

12. Floor statement by Sen. Jeremiah Denton, June 20, 1983.

11

The Guns Of Gaberone— SA Raids the ANC

The Nkomati accord signed by Marxist Mozambique and South Africa forced the terrorist African National Congress (ANC) out of Mozambique. This was a serious setback for the ANC since it depends on foreign bases to support terrorist activity inside South Africa. Its removal from Mozambique closed a prime infiltration route into South Africa.

It soon became clear to intelligence agencies in South Africa that the ANC was looking elsewhere and had began establishing infiltration routes from Botswana. This was confirmed by an upswing in terrorist incidents inside South Africa, especially in the Western Transvaal and Cape Province areas adjacent to Botswana. When President Masire of Botswana gave the ANC permission to operate a political office in his country he brought a cobra into the house as a pet. The devious ANC leader Oliver Tambo took advantage of Masire's misguided hospitality and sent a secret message to ANC members in Botswana placing them on "full-scale" armed alert" with orders to continue terrorist acts against South Africa from there.

As terrorism rose in South Africa, Pretoria began to bitterly protest against the ANC havens in Botswana. Pushed for an explanation by the Botswana government, Tambo assured it that ANC members there were nothing more than innocent refugees, and that no terrorist activities were planned or launched from Botswana. However, South African agents intercepted a secret dispatch from Tambo to ANC cadres hiding in Gaberone, Botswana's capital, urging them to ignore what he had said publicly and continue their

An assassin's weapon: A silencer-equipped AK-47 Soviet-made assault rifle seized during the Gaberone raid.

A sophisticated telescopic night-sight for the Soviet-made RPG-7 rocket launcher, a favorite terrorist weapon.

A collection of terrorist weapons seized during the raid on Gaberone. The presence of these weapons refutes the claim that the raid site housed refugees.

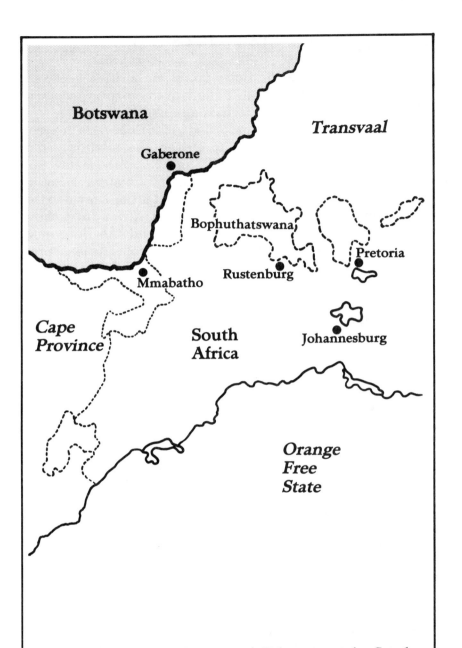

Map showing the proximity of Gaberone to the South African border. The ANC "activiated" Botswana as a springboard for Terrorist Attacks on the Republic of South Africa.

planned activities. Still, Botswana's authorities accepted Tambo's lies and let the ANC remain in the country, where it continued its murderous activities against South Africa.

South African officials protested to the Botswana government, repeatedly warning it to curtail the planning and execution of terrorist activities by the ANC. "The Botswana government has," South African Foreign Minister Pik Botha said, "on a number of occasions had its attention drawn to the infiltration of ANC terrorists into South Africa from third countries through Botswana territory, and the Botswana government has been requested to take appropriate measures to prevent this infiltration."[1]

Indeed, officials from the governments of both countries met repeatedly over the matter of ANC sanctuaries in Botswana. During one such meeting, on April 21, 1983, held in Jan Smuts Airport outside Johannesburg, the Botswana government was given a list of ANC terrorists in Botswana, along with details of their participation in terrorist acts against South Africa. Botswana was strongly urged to take "appropriate action" to curtail ANC activities.

A year later, in March 1984, the South African government proposed, and the Botswana government accepted, that the security forces of the two countries should design measures to prevent the planning and execution of acts of violence, sabotage and terrorism against each other. On May 24, 1984, another meeting was held in Pretoria where a consensus was apparently reached that neither country would harbor groups planning terrorism. The "apparent" consensus soon cease to exist as ANC terrorists continued to operate out of Botswana.

In a public statement on September 12, 1984, Pik Botha said the Botswana government had not been able to reach an acceptable understanding with the South African government on the terrorism issue. He "therefore warned that South Africa reserved the right to take steps to prevent acts of terror and sabotage from being planned and executed from neighboring states."[2] South Africa had already demonstrated its willingness to launch commando raids against ANC terrorist bases in neighboring countries. Three raids, for example, had been carried out in Mozambique, and another in Maseru,

Lesotho. Botswana was clearly warned that similar action would be forthcoming if the ANC continued using Botswana's territory to launch terrorist attacks against South Africa.

After this warning, security forces of both countries held another meeting in Gaberone, Botswana's capital, on October 30 that ended without result because Botswana's security authorities had no mandate from their government to work with the South Africans. (The logical question is: Then why go to the meeting?) Whatever their differences, the two countries were trying to settle the problem. But the ANC continued operating from Botswana, in particular, from Gaberone, only 20 kilometers from the Tlokwenge Gate, the border post with South Africa.

For the ANC, Gaberone was a strategically important location. Having an international air terminal, it was easily accessible from most other points on the globe and even closer to South Africa than the ANC base in Mozambique's capital, Maputo. And despite complaints by the South Africans, the Botswana government turned a blind eye on ANC activity. It was an intolerable situation for the South Africans.

Still, South Africa preferred the diplomatic route. During discussions between the South African police and Botswana police in Gaberone on January 24, 1985, Botswana was again warned that there was conclusive evidence that the ANC was using Botswana as a launching pad for terrorism inside South Africa. In a telex five days later, Pik Botha again stressed the need for effective arrangements between the two security forces. Stating that terrorism against South Africa and its neighbor, the Republic of Bophuthatswana, had increased, Botha again pointed out that "... peace and stability in southern Africa could not be maintained if terrorists and their supporters, intent on the overthrow by force of the sovereign government, were harboured in the territory of a neighboring state, be it with or without that state's knowledge or consent. In short, the situation cannot continue."[3]

Finally, the foreign ministers of both countries met in Pretoria on February 22, 1985, to make an arrangement between the security forces of both countries that neither would be used as a terrorist base. "The Botswana Foreign Minister was told that South Africa knew for a fact that the ANC had chosen Botswana as an important infiltration route to South Africa," Botha said. "It was agreed during this meeting that the security forces of the two countries would once again attempt to come to an understanding of practical arrangements on how to combat this growing danger.

"However, at a meeting between the security forces of the two countries which followed, the Botswana security forces again indicated that they had no mandate to accept the proposed arrangement, though they themselves displayed a willingness to do so because of a realization on their part of the destabilizing effect of the growing ANC presence in Botswana." Thus Botswana's government, although aware of the danger posed by ANC terrorists, was reluctant to take action against them, because they feared retaliation from the radical black African leaders for cooperating with the South Africans.

Early in the summer of 1985 South African intelligence learned of a terrorist attack timed to coincide with a 10-day international conference of the ANC at a secret venue somewhere in Africa. The campaign was to consist of a series of attacks and assassination attempts on moderate Black and Colored leaders in South Africa. The strategy was made in Botswana.[4] The plot was discovered by painstaking undercover surveillance, interception of communications and infiltration of the ANC by South African intelligence agents.

On June 12, 1985, the ANC launched two attacks in Cape Town that fell in line with the plan detected by South African intelligence. Grenade attacks on Mr. Luwellwyn Landers, a Colored Deputy Minister-designate, and another Colored member of Parliament in Cape Town, were the first shots fired in the ANC campaign. This was the last straw for the South Africans, who decided to retaliate against the ANC and carry out a raid on known ANC targets in Gaberone. In the early hours of the morning, just two days after the grenade attack in Cape Town, they struck the ANC in Gaberone. The targets were ten houses and offices spread throughout Gaberone in such a way that the ANC could hide, or so they thought, in residential and business areas of town. From these hideouts, apparently peaceful inhabitants formed the control center of ANC activities in the Transvaal sabotage organization, claimed General Constand Viljoen, then Chief of the South African Defense Force, whose members took part, along with the South African Police, in the Gaberone raid.

He said that some of the targets had been involved in providing a "crash course" for ANC terrorists. Previously, the ANC would establish bases where terrorist trainees would spend lengthy periods under instruction. But since the bases in Gaberone and elsewhere in Botswana were easily detectable, such crash courses had been devised for the would-be terrorist. Recruits would arrive in Botswana ostensibly as normal weekend tourists, but they received training in subjects such as the handling of grenades. The Palestine Liberation Organization (PLO) has been involved in training ANC terrorists for some time. Grenade attacks upon civilians are a favorite PLO tactic. The grenade attacks on the two Cape Town politicians showed that the pupils had learned their lessons.

The Gaberone raid wasn't aimed at the government or the people of Botswana, but at clearly identified militant terrorists planning violence and murder in the Republic of South Africa. South African intelligence was thorough—its commandos had photos of the targeted terrorists so that positive identification could be made before an attack. The raiders took every precaution to ensure the safety of innocents—they used hand-held, battery-powered amplifiers to warn people in the vicinity to stay inside. Only known terrorists would be attacked.

"There were cases," General Viljoen said, "where women in the houses were saved because they were identified as not being terrorists. Unfortunately, also in the crossfire, according to our records at this stage, one woman and two children were wounded. According to Botswana radio, one child died. That is a great pity."[5]

"The loss of innocent life is deeply regretted," Pik Botha said in a letter to his counterpart in Botswana. "I trust that you will reciprocate this sentiment in respect of the lives of inncoent people killed and murdered in South Africa as a result of ANC terrorism emanating from Botswana."

Captured material and weapons were highly specialized. One item, which normally is not used by the military, not to mention innocent civilians, as apologists called the dead ANC terrorists, was an AK-47 assault rifle fitted with a silencer. This, along with subsonic ammunition, was found at one of the raid sites. Another sophisticated item was an optical sight for the Soviet-made RPG rocket launcher, a favorite terrorist weapon. In daylight, it can be used as a telescopic sight, and at night, a battery-illuminated reticule allows it to be used in the darkness. Pistols, hand grenades, rifles and detailed instructions on how to make and detonate car bombs were also found.

The commandos also seized thousands of documents described as a "treasure trove of intelligence." The most important find was the ANC's financial records from Botswana, dating from 1977. They contained full details of receipts, payments and records of subscriptions which, supported by other documents, showed that the ANC in Botswana ran a bank account under the name "African Arts and Crafts Exporting Agents." Among the equipment and documents was a small computer used by the Solidarity News Service. Major Craig Williamson of the South African police was a co-founder of the "news service" after he infiltrated the ANC as an operative based in Gaberone.

"We started it as the South African News Service in those days,"[6] he said. The service was a front for ANC intelligence and propaganda. Other items, such as floppy disks containing the names and records of ANC members in Botswana and South Africa, were also captured. The documents also verified ANC involvement in some South African trade unions and the United Democratic Front, a group popular with American liberals. Seized telephone accounts reported calls to Luanda and numerous ANC contacts in South Africa.

Specifically, the documents revealed:

- That the ANC was considering becoming involved with the youth of Botswana, who were politically "vague and ill-informed";
- ANC manuals containing instructions and strategy for instigating school boycotts as a part of a political action "against the system";

- Memos indicating a move to recruit "white activists" involved in "anti-conscription" activities into the ANC;
- Long-playing records, manufactured in Holland and Sweden, exhorting ANC members to kill people in Pretoria;
- Plans, including photographs of the intended target, for attacking a house in Bophuthatswana.

In short, material captured in Gaberone provided overwhelming proof that the South African decision to carry out the raid was a prudent one. "This has shown us that the ANC was not involved in Botswana operations since only yesterday," Major Williamson said. "We can equate what the ANC is doing in Gaberone to what the PLO has done in Beirut. They are acting in a clandestine manner to carry out acts of terror."[7]

As could be expected, the raid gave South Africa another black eye and drew unmitigated world-wide criticism, especially from the sanctimonious capitals of Washington and London. The Reagan Administration recalled Ambassador Herman Nickel for "consultations." State Department spokesman Bernard Kalb said the Gaberone raid was "particularly deplorable" in light of progress made by Botswana and the South African government to control cross-border violence.

British reaction was much the same. South Africa's ambassador to Great Britain was summoned to the Foreign Office and told of the Thatcher government's "concern and shock." He pointed out the "irrefutable proof" that Botswana was being used by the ANC as an infiltration route and that numerous acts of terrorism had been traced to the ANC in Botswana. British Foreign Secretary Geoffrey Howe said that wherever violence occurred it was deplorable, an odd statement in view of the fact that the State Department and British Foreign Office are mostly silent about ANC terrorism.

The self-righteous comments of Washington and London notwithstanding, it was clear that Botswana, lacking the political courage to deal with the ANC, would do nothing to stop the Soviet-backed terrorists in their midst. Thus, the South Africans had two options: 1) continue useless talking with Botswana while the ANC continued its reign of terror, or 2) take care of the problem themselves.

1. *The* (Johannesburg) *Star* (June 14, 1985), p. 1.
2. Ibid.
3. "Botswana Had Been Warned," *Paratus* (July 1985), p. 21. *The Star* (June 14, 1985), p. 1.
4. Ibid., (*The Star*) p. 3.
5. "ANC Terror Hide-Out Destroyed," *Paratus* (July 1985), p. 19.
6. *The Star* (June 21, 1985), p. 13.
7. Ibid.

The Voortrekker Memorial in Pretoria, commemorating the Great Trek migration of the Afrikaaner into the interior of South Africa.

Farmers in southern Africa are fortifying their farms against armed terrorist attacks.

12

The Republic Of South Africa—
A Multi-Ethnic Society

South Africa has always been considered a nation with cultural, as well as economic, political and strategic ties to the West. It fought on the allied side in both World Wars and contributed to U.S.-led U.N. forces in Korea. Of late, however, it has been the target of a get-South-Africa campaign because apartheid is one of the cornerstones of government policy. But few who have spent so much time riding the hate-South-Africa bandwagon understand what apartheid is, its theoretical foundations, or why, in fact, they should be against it (although almost everyone is).

In Afrikaans, the lingua-franca of South Africa, apartheid literally means "apartness." It is a race-related policy inaugurated in 1948 that outlawed intermingling of the races, established white supremacy in the marketplace, and segregated the black population. The segregation was accomplished by confining blacks to tribal areas, or homelands, and controlling the movement of black workers into cities and towns. Political control has remained in white hands as only whites are allowed to vote.

To Americans just recently finished with the process of emancipation of fellow black citizens, this policy is abhorrent. Our attitude toward South Africa is influenced by our attitude toward blacks that evolved from the American civil rights movement of the 1960s. South Africa is, however, neither an American nor European society. Nor is South Africa unique —in many ways, it is a typical Africa country that responds to endemic problems in a typical African manner.

The single most dominant characteristic of the African

continent is its lack of racial, cultural and linguistic unity. No other continent is so fragmented by so many different ethnic groups. Hundreds of years of colonialism on the African continent brought together and transformed many tribal societies into 50 superficially modern states, which, since the Second World War, have been independent from their colonial overlords. Not one country is homogeneous. Even the smallest, like Rwanda, are split by tribal and racial fissures. The world has witnessed appalling violent, bloody civil wars in Nigeria, the Sudan, Chad, Zaire, Uganda, Angola, Mozambique and elsewhere.

South Africa is no exception. Her ethnic divisions are large and more complex than a simple black versus white situation, although the radical left would have us believe otherwise. South African blacks are not an homogeneous group—they have no ethnic unity, and are subdivided into four main cultural-linguistic groups. Each subdivision can in turn be subdivided into separate ethnic groups, each with its own language, legal system, lifestyle, values and socio-political structures.

America has little to compare with this diversity, although American Indians are a remote analogy. An equally remote analogy, but one that can give a reader an insight into the problem of tribalism throughout Africa, is ethnic neighborhoods in large American cities. In such neighborhoods, the language and customs of the old country are preserved. Residents generally keep to themselves. Italians, Irish, Chinese and Polish Americans often live in areas completely dominated by one ethnic group. Rarely do these groups cross lines out of their respective neighborhoods.

In Africa, a similar, but more intense situation exists. Instead of ignoring or, in the worst case, chasing a stranger out of the neighborhood, the African may resort to more serious forms of expressing disapproval of stangers, as recent tribal clashes there indicate.

****

A quick look at the racial composition of South Africa reveals some significant facts:

The Zulus, with almost seven million people, are the largest racial group in South Africa. They are further divided into about 200 tribes, each of which can be subdivided further into clans. The next largest group is the whites, numbering about five million. They too, are composed of ethnic groups: Dutch, English, French and German. The two distinct white cultures and languages are Afrikaans and English. Other important sub-groups are the Jews, Portuguese, Greeks, Italians and, more recently, a large number of Rhodesian whites. Though English-speaking, they too have cultural values different from their South African cousins.

Third in size are the Xhosa (pronounced "Causa"), with nearly three million members; followed by the mixed-race group called Coloreds, slightly fewer in number than the Xhosa; the North Sotho, with 2.3 million members; South Sotho, with 1.8 million; and the Tswana, with 1.2 million.

There are seven other groups, ranging from the Shangaan, numbering 890,000, to Asians, with 870,000 and the Venda, with 209,000. This last group is the most homogeneous black ethnic group, although it has 27 distinct tribes.

Sixty-five percent of the Asians are Hindus, 21 percent Muslims. Christians, Buddhists and other religions make up the rest.

Excluding those spoken by whites, there are four major and 23 minor languages spoken by blacks in South Africa.

Talk about diversity, South Africa has it with a vengeance. Yet the country mirrors the rest of the continent: It is rich in cultural and ethnic diversity. African governments cope with this diversity by means of social engineering in which individual rights are sacrificed to so-called group rights, which usually means the fancy of the tribe in power. People are treated not as individuals, but as sheep to be pushed around in herds.

This social engineering is conducted on a tribal basis since the continent is so lacking homogeneity; one tribe can lord it over the rest. And South Africa is no different from the rest of the continent in this respect.

There is not a single African country where tribal or racial origins, skin color or religious affiliation are not of prime importance in securing elemental political or economic rights. The western concept of one man, one vote is understood, in general, by African politicians not as a means of peaceably transferring power over a period of time but a seizing and holding of power indefinitely.

The American philosopher Richard Weaver once said: "Ideas have consequences." The African experience bears out Weaver's observation. Most African politico-social theories are variants of socialism or despotic dictatorships. In this context, all African states are, in differing degrees, racist. Almost without exception, all practice discrimination against some group: Jews, whites, Asians, non-Muslim religious groups or disfavored tribes. Thus, a wide variety of discriminatory practices have been codified into legal systems throughout the continent. Many have taken the form of a strange brand of socialism or social policy.

Tanzania, for example, is governed by a particularly sinister doctrine called Ujauma; Ghana has its Consciencism; there is the Zambiam doctrine of Humanism, and Negritude is practiced in Senegal. Zaire is more honest, and calls its ruling doctrine Mobutuism, after the dictator of the same name. Most of these doctrines were cooked up in the political science or sociology departments of local universities. All reflect the desires or whims of the ruling racial group.

Apartheid is no different. It is a philosophy developed in the social-psychology department of Stellenbosch University, the last bastion of the hard-core Afrikaaner. Apartheid, as do many of the other doctrines mentioned above, represents and protects the interests of the ruling group—in this instance Dutch-Afrikaaners—just as Ujauma represents the interests of Nyerere's regime in Tanzania.

Apartheid exploits blacks economically, denies them political rights, segregates them and is enforced by a heavy-handed state bureaucracy. On the other hand, tribal or Marxist governments in black Africa run their economies into ruin, though occasionally giving people a vote—either a choice of a dictated one-party slate or coerced in a particular direction as in Zimbabwe. These black tyrants humiliate and oppress their tribal opponents, torture political prisoners, use police and troops to inflict genocidal policies of mass murder, and give their elites privileges that are abused in ways never dreamed of by the most recalcitrant racist Afrikaaner politician.

All of this goes on, yet there is not a single peep of protest by those who daily condemn the crumbling South African policy of apartheid. "Oh, but you see," our hate-South-African spokesman will say, "apartheid is worse because a man can't change the color of his skin, and that is the sole criterion of judgment under apartheid." But in black Africa where murder, torture, mayhem and other human rights violations are the order of the day, a man cannot change his tribal birth either. In the vast majority of the continent he is trapped by this as surely as by skin color in South Africa, with less hope of relief through reforms and progress than are offered by the current South African government.

Recently, the South African government began the laborious process of dismantling apartheid, which requires a huge, clumsy bureaucracy to enforce it. The fact that 10 million blacks live and work in areas officially designated "white only" shows that the physical core, "apartness," has been crumbling. South Africa also has done away with laws banning interracial marriage. And most recently, it abolished the hated "pass-laws," which required blacks to carry identification cards when they traveled. This will be replaced by a system that requires all South Africans to carry identification papers.

It is quite clear, the Western liberal media notwithstanding, that South African leader P.W. Botha is convinced that apartheid must go. He has been slowly making reforms so as to avoid panic in the ruling National Party. Unlike other African leaders, Botha has an electorate to which he must answer. He is not a dictator like fellow leaders on the African continent. The question remains: Will the change be peaceable and evolutionary, or violent—in the words of the proponents of violence, "revolutionary." That is the dilemma facing South Africa.

Gatsha Buthelezi, head of the Zulu nation, argues for peaceful change: "If change is ever achieved in South Africa through violence, we will find that the foundations of the future will have been destroyed in the course of liberating the country. . . . I believe ways and means can be found to build up the black bargaining power to force whites to the negotiating table. . . . For the vast majority of blacks, the struggle has always been for inclusion in the existing South Africa; it has always been a struggle to transform the state rather than destroy and rebuild it."[1]

On the other hand, the proponents of violent revolutionary change reject Buthelezi's method. Indeed, groups like the Marxist-dominated African National Congress are doing everything in their power to murder or terrorize their way into power in South Africa.

Harmony and peace among all groups in South Africa is possible if, as Buthelezi said, the groups negotiate to change South African society and rebuild it, not destroy it. For it is out of the chaos of revolutionary change, with the willing connivance of Western liberals, that the Soviet-Mongols hope to establish their hegemony over Southern Africa.

1. "The Only Road to Liberation," *The Washington Post* (October 28, 1984), p. 7.

13

South Africa: Soviet-Mongol Target

The great difference between the Republic of South Africa and the rest of the continent is that South Africa, to a degree, has a free enterprise economy. It enjoys the only modern economy on the continent and thus is the crown jewel to be captured by the Soviet block in southern Africa—it has both strategic minerals and the Cape of Good Hope.

But the Soviet Union has an ample supply of minerals in its own territory and could cut the Cape sea route without possessing South Africa (although the job would be easier if Simons Town were a Soviet naval base). So why have they targeted South Africa for conquest?

Three reasons are evident. First, although the Soviets don't need minerals from South Africa, the U.S. and NATO do. The Soviets want to deprive the West of this mineral treasure chest. Second, control of South Africa would complete the USSR's quest for military control of the entire region, allowing the Soviets easy access to strategic ports on the Indian and Atlantic Oceans and unrestricted access to the Cape route. The last and perhaps most significant reason is that socialism survives by parasitism. The Soviets need the rich, vibrant South African economy to support their vassals in Angola, Mozambique and other countries.

Zimbabwe is a good example. Although not strictly a member of the Soviet Empire, Mugabe has made no secret of his desire to turn the country into a one-party Marxist-Leninist dictatorship. Since he began to move in that direction, he has turned Zimbabwe's once productive economy into chaos. Only strong economic ties with South Africa keep Zimbabwe above water.

A prominent American Marxist-Leninist theoretician,

Rod Bush, writing in a special issue of *The Journal of Contemporary Marxism*, in an article entitled "Proletarianization and Class Struggle in Africa," said: "Revolutionary change in South Africa will change not only the face of southern Africa as a region, but also the balance of forces on the entire continent and among the core powers of the world system. *A revolutionary government in South Africa could use the country's highly-developed industrial base to provide significant material support to Angola, Mozambique and Guinea-Bissau, as well as to revolutionary governments in Zimbabwe and Namibia* [emphasis added]. A block of such revolutionary nation states in southern Africa would greatly maximize the possibility of a socialist construction in those states and in other parts of the world system. . . . That is a sobering thought to give pause to all of us."[1]

Bush readily admits that South Africa's economy would help the sick socialist economies of Southern Africa. What Bush and other socialists never talk about are the consequences of the socialization of yet another country. When Bush and his friends finish with South Africa, they will have ruined the only economy that could have sustained any economic growth beneficial to the region. What happens to South Africa's economy has a profound effect on the region. It is the most industrialized and diversified economy on the whole African continent, dwarfing its neighbors in energy production, transportation needs, goods produced and research and development.

For example, although South Africa boasts only six percent of the continent's population and three percent of its land, it produces 25 percent of the continent's goods, 40 percent of industrial machinery, 45 percent of its mined goods, 77 percent of its electricity, 46 percent of its motor vehicles (there are more black-owned cars in South Africa than privately-owned cars in the Soviet Union), 36 percent of its telephones, and 40 percent of its corn, the staple of most Africans. In short, South Africa has a First World economy on a Third World Continent.

The strength of South Africa's economy is even more evident when compared with those of its neighbors, many of which are poverty-stricken outposts of the Red Empire or socialist wastelands.

South Africa employs more than 300,000 blacks from neighboring states. One of the six leading food exporters in the world, South Africa provides food, consumer and capital goods for its neighbors and carries a sizable portion of their goods destined for world markets.

About half of South Africa's black miners come from abroad and send their wages home. About 10 million people in a half-dozen countries are financially dependent on South Africa's mining industry. Its breakdown would cause an unimaginable catastrophe for the whole of southern Africa. Black Africans, like other people, vote most sincerely with their feet—South Africa is the country many prefer to work and live in. They reject, vividly, the heaven of socialism and flock in droves to the alleged hell of apartheid.

South Africa's 1980 per capita income of $2,290 was eight times that of Mozambique's, four times that of Zambia's, and 3.6 times that of Zimbabwe's which, when these figures were compiled, had yet to be turned over to the ministrations of Robert Mugabe. Zimbabwe's economy is approaching the lows of its neighbors.

South Africa's contribution to the continent's economy is truly incredible:

- 77 percent of total Gross National Product;
- 77 percent of the electricity generated;
- 84 percent of installed telephones;
- 97 percent of the mined coal;
- 82 percent of the mined chrome;
- 70 percent of the corn grown;
- 87 percent of the wheat grown;
- 67 percent of the sugar cane grown;
- 39 percent of the cattle raised.

South Africa dominates the transportation industy in southern Africa. Eight of the fourteen countries in southern Africa are landlocked and depend upon railroads to carry their goods to seaports mainly located in South Africa for shipment to overseas markets. South African railroads handle the bulk of Zaire's, Zambia's and Zimbabwe's foreign trade. Approximately 70 percent of Zambia's rail cargo moves through South Africa in spite of the TanZam railroad built by the Chinese Communists to bypass railroads running through white-ruled Rhodesia. At least 60 percent of Malawi's exports go through South Africa, as do 60 percent of Zimbabwe's imports and exports.

Contacts between railway officials and transport services of the countries follow normal business principles as if no friction existed between South Africa and her neighbors.

In short, while radical leftist southern African leaders rail against South Africa publicly, they work quitely behind the scenes with the "racist regime" to keep the regional economy running.

A recent example highlights the hypocrisy. Shortly after the long dormant Beira to Mutare oil pipeline was repaired and placed in service in August 1982, anti-communist RENA-MO troops in Mozambique blew up fuel storage tanks near Beira, effectively stopping the flow of fuel to Zimbabawe. Adding to the crisis was the fact that Zimbabwe had ceased the importation of fuel from South Africa. Thus, Zimbabwe had an immediate fuel shortage.

A temporary solution to the problem came about after the Zimbabwean National Railway Administration approached its South African counterparts, requesting the movement of high capacity oil-tank cars from Beit Bridge on the South Africa-Zimbabwe border, to Komatipoort on the South Africa-Mozambique border. The plan involved the use of South African rail lines and equipment. Oil from Mozambique was loaded onto tank cars and shipped through South Africa into Zimbabwe via the Beit Bridge route. While this commercial movement of fuel was taking place, the Zimbabwean government was busy blaming South Africa for regional unrest.

South Africa is blessed with one of the richest and most varied ranges of natural resources in the world. It has one of the richest deposits of minerals. It exports almost all of what it mines (about 85 percent) and is the world's largest supplier of gold, platinum, gem diamonds, chrome, vanadium, manganese, andalusite metal, vermiculite and asbestos fibers. It is the second largest supplier of uranium and antimony and ranks in the top ten suppliers of nickel, copper, tin, silver, coal and fluorspar. It has 86 percent of the free-world's platinum-group metals, 64 percent of its vanadium, 48 percent of its manganese ore, 83 percent of its chrome ore and nearly 50 percent of its gold.

The mineral wealth of South Africa is vital to the survival of the West, as noted earlier. Western industry is dependent on South Africa's chrome, manganese, vanadium and platinum. A major disruption in this mineral supply would have a disastrous impact on oil refining, steel production, the machine tool industry and our space program. In short, everything from refrigerators to space shuttles would be affected by a loss of our South African mineral supply.

****

A cursory glance at the economic travails of the rest of Africa will explain Soviet action in southern Africa. The Soviets' Marxist-Leninist policies have wrecked not only Mother Russia, but every country unlucky enough to find itself part of the Soviet-Mongol colonial empire.

The *Economist* of London has pointed out that "it takes the acts of men to turn acts of God into calamity. In Ethiopia, local drought has been followed, as it always is, by local shortages of food. Farmers on the fragile soils of Africa know all about that. Left to themselves, they save in good years for the bad seasons that are bound to come. But the Ethiopian junta has forbidden that. In place of a bad old regime run by grasping and incompetent landlords, Colonel Mengistu Haile Mariam and his colleagues have installed a bad new regime, run by doctrinaire and incompetent soldiers. Saving food from good years is called hoarding. Saving money earned from past harvests is called capitalist accumulation. Earning a living transporting food is called exploitation. All are punished by official extortion or worse. That was how Stalin choked off farming in the Soviet Union where it has still not recovered. . . ."[2]

As former U.S. Ambassador to the UN Jeane Kirkpatrick has pointed out, "Many parts of the continent, including areas that were previously net food exporters, have become dependent on food imports. . . . Coercion has failed where market incentives might have succeeded."[3]

Africa, with the exception of South Africa, is the only part of the world growing less food than it grew 20 years ago. In Ghana, for example, Kwame Nkrumah, the father of African nationalism, following a socialist model, nationalized the tobacco industry, with predictable results. The country's 1984 tobacco production was one-tenth what it was in 1974. Ghana's cocoa crop, for 67 years the world's largest, fell to about 270,000 tons in 1984 from 440,000 tons just after independence. As pointed out by Dr. Melvin B. Krause of the Hoover Institution, "Ghana would appear to be an example par excellence of a Third World country where socialism and the welfare state have made totalitarianism a recurrent aspect of political life." He could easily have named Angola, Mozambique or Zimbabwe.

In the People's Republic of Congo, to cite one more glaring example, sugar output at the Suco sugar plantation, nationalized in 1970, fell so much that it was shut down in 1977. The same story can be told elsewhere in Africa wherever the disease of socialism has poisoned a country's economy.

The socialist state's only method of survival, as mentioned earlier, is to be a parasite on some rich state. There is no richer state on the African continent than the Republic of South Africa. It is the healthy body the parasitic socialist states of Africa need to feed on. This is the reason, above others, why the Soviet-Mongols are making such a concerted effort to destabilize the country and to install a Marxist government in South Africa. The Marxist-Leninist ideology that holds them in its iron grip does not permit them to resort to the obvious use of the hated capitalistic system to feed and clothe their subjects. Their ideology demands that it be imposed by force and violence. It cannot do otherwise. The very nature of socialism—that the state shall be empowered to regulate peoples' every activity and confiscate all their property—demands violent action. The success of any socialist program depends on only one thing: who has more firepower, the socialists or their enemies.

Why will death and starvation result from the absorption of South Africa into the Soviet colonial empire? Socialism represents the ultimate growth of government. Governments, however, are not entrepreneurs, they cannot create wealth and progress. All governments can do is direct resources from some uses into other uses. Governments do not wave magic wands; instead they point guns at the heads of their citizens in order to extort money and property out of them. Socialism not only extorts money at the point of a gun, it extorts everything a citizen owns. Therefore, socialism does not—and cannot—build up the capital or individual entrepreneurial spirit necessary to keep an economy running properly. It seeks only to expropriate or destroy the capital, property and individuality of others. As such, it exalts a malignant, misanthropic disposition and turns it into a vicious machine for tyranny.

It is South Africa's economic wealth, more than its strategic position, that is coveted by its communist enemies. The Soviet Union needs South Africa's vibrant economy to support is economically prostrate, far-flung African empire.

1. *The Journal of Contemporary Marxism*, No. 6 (Spring 1983).

2. Quoted in "The Independent Black States of Southern Africa," American African Affairs Association, Washington, D.C. (1984), p. 24.

3. Ibid.

4. Ibid., p. 25.

14

The Regeneration of South Africa

Just as the Messianic ideology of Marxism-Leninism is guiding the Soviet Union's missionary quest in southern Africa, so it is that Christianity may save the region from its ever-approaching dismal fate.

Whatever else one may think about South Africa, religious tolerance is widespread. There are no restrictions on any form of worship and all South African schools begin their day with prayer, something our "democratic" society will not permit. The vast majority of South Africans, black and white, are Christians. Eighty-five percent of the black community professes some form of Christian allegiance. Further, the majority of these worshippers could be classified as fundamentalists since they accept the literal interpretation of the Bible as God's word. Like the American experience, South Africa's fundamentalist growth has come at the expense of "mainline" churches.

Also as in the United States, it is liberal spokesmen from these mainline churches who presume to speak for Christians in both countries. The South African Council of Churches, ideological soulmate of the U.S. National Council of Churches, is presumed to represent all Christian churches in South Africa. In fact, rank and file individual church members are often appalled by the policies advocated in their names by the Council of Churches and have little recourse except to leave a member church and worhip elsewhere.

The Council of Churches in both the U.S. and South Africa are radical organizations supportive of left-wing causes ranging from the ANC to nuclear freeze. Both groups frequently give more weight to their causes than is justified, merely because they appear to speak with great moral

authority. Thus, we have the obnoxious spectacle of the
Bishop of Cape Town, Desmond Tutu, former head of the
South African Council of Churches, and Allen Boesak, its
current leader, preaching revolutionary violence to the wild
applause of friends in the liberal media. These two men have
little or no support among the majority of South African
blacks.

Nineteen denominations are affiliated with the South
African Council of Churches, equaling about one million
members. Neither the three Afrikaaner churches nor the
Roman Catholic church is a member. By contrast, the Dutch
Reformed Church alone boasts 1.7 million members, and it is
only one denomination, nor is it a member of the South
African Council of Churches.

The Black Zionist Christian Church represents three
million members. Its Easter Service, the largest in Christen-
dom, draws more than three million people from all over
southern Africa. The black Christian Reformed Independent
Churches Association, under the leadership of Bishop Issac
Mokoena, represents 864 black churches with a combined
membership of about 4.5 million. Both groups have several
times the number of members of the South African Council of
Churches, which is routinely represented as the majority
voice for South African religious opinion, both black and
white. Neither group belongs to the South African Council of
Churches.

"[The] suggestion that there is an appearance of international support for the ANC does not represent the sentiments
of Black Christians in South Africa," said Bishop Mokena.
"People who are carrying out the request for financial support
for the ANC are not speaking for the Reformed Independent
Churches Association with its 4.5 million Black Christians
over the age of 15 years. They are also not speaking on behalf
of the Zion Christian Church with its 6 million adherents, nor
are they speaking on behalf of Chief Gatsha Buthelezi of
Inkatha, who has repeatedly rejected the ANC as a terrorist
organization.

"The money that you have does not belong to you,"
Mokena stressed. "You are mere administrators of God's
funds. And if you are not going to take account to see as to how

these monies are used, you are answerable before God on Judgment Day. Because these monies are being used to stimulate war amongst Blacks; so many lives have been lost! Most of the Black people who have died in our Black townships have died at the hands of their so-called liberators who are not ashamed to act like cannibals. What happens in our townships is something that has been imported from somewhere else. It is not Black-oriented. It is not South African-oriented either, And, therefore, it is just unfortunate that it happened to be the men of the frock who want to stimulate this kind of war by going further and asking for international financial support of an organization that is not geared at fighting against their suppressors, who are white, but go back into the townships to exterminate their own fellow Christians, their own Black brothers."[1]

It is the Christian faith, not the liberation theology taught by Tutu and Boesek, that will provide the common ground on which blacks and whites in South Africa can meet and peacefully resolve their differences. Before that day comes, great theological difficulties must be overcome. The first step must be taken by the Calvinist Dutch Reformed Church, since it was a corruption of the Calvinist faith that led to the rise of apartheid, and thus to many of South Africa's problems.

****

South Africa's first white settlers were primarily Dutch Protestants or French Huguenots fleeing religious persecution in Catholic France during the seventeenth century. Both groups were staunchly Protestant and steeped in the doctrine of Protestantism advanced by John Calvin. They carried with them to South Africa a tradition of dissent and a dose of resentment against European ways.

Their Calvinism constituted a world and life view based upon their understanding of Scripture. Their highly individualistic society reflected this. It was based on the law of God as revealed in the scriptures. The rules they enacted to govern their society—its laws—also had to be grounded in the Biblical scriptures. The result was a society that permitted maximum flexibility, or individual freedom if you will—but within the moral framework of their Calvinist doctrine. It was sort of an "anything goes" attitude, as long as it was done within the guidelines of their Biblical-based society.

The whites, not only in South Africa but other European colonizing powers, looked upon the natives in their far-flung colonies as "heathen folk." These "heathen folk" were the target of missionary evangelism and the important first step in the "civilizing" process of the natives was their conversion to Christianity—conversion first, civilizing later. In most of the European colonies the step from conversion to full-fledged participation in society progressed slowly, if at all. In most it didn't take place until after the Second World War.

The most fervent defenders of the Calvinist faith in South Africa were the Trekboers, the nomadic farmers, whose search for new grazing lands took them deeper and deeper into South Africa's interior. These hardy souls literally moved into the interior with a musket in one hand and their ever-present Bible in the other.

Facing disease, the whims of a fickle weather, and the raiding depredations of the natives they encountered, tempered these hardy pioneers into a tough, independent, God-fearing patriarchical society. Their cousins who remained in the Cape Colony, while not pioneers like the Trekboers, still retained their individualistic outlook on life. They as well as the Trekboers, were not friendly towards other European cultural influences upon their way of life. Unfortunately, the storm clouds gathering over Europe would bring profound changes upon them. The Little Corporal was on the march against established order in Europe.

During his reign, Napoleon put members of his family on the thrones of the countries he conquered, one of which was in Holland. Unfortunately for the Dutch, this placed them on the losing side in the Napoleonic wars. For this sin, Great Britain, as part of the spoils of war, took permanent possession of the Cape because of its strategic importance in protecting the sea route to British India and points East. The British quickly imposed Crown rule upon the Afrikaaner residents in their new colony, a move much resented by the individualist-minded Afrikaaners.

In 1822, the British colonial governor, Lord Charles Somerset, issued a decree that English was to be the only language of the courts and schools, even though Dutch-speaking settlers outnumbered the English eight to one. Afrikaaners, or Boers, as they were called in the 1800s, responded by moving away from their new British masters. The Great Trek, an important part of South African history, was the exodus, from 1835-37, of over 5,000 Boers across the Orange and Vaal rivers well beyond, they hoped, British meddling. They set up two independent Boer republics, the Republic Transvaal and the Orange Free State. This trek to the interior was their means of preserving Afrikaaner culture and community from British influence.

But the British doggedly pursued them. In May 1843 the Crown annexed Natal on the Indian Ocean as one of her colonies. The hoisting of the Union Jack in Port Natal (present-day Durban), was the final straw for many of the Boers who had moved there on the Great Trek a few years earlier. Packing their belongings into ox-drawn covered wagons, three-quarters of the Boer settlers in Natal went west over the Dragensberg mountains to settle in the two Boer republics.

But the British still would not leave them in peace. In 1852, Britain recognized the Republic of Transvaal, allowing the Boers to govern it according to their own laws. As part of the agreement, the Republic of Transvaal abolished slavery. Two years later, in 1854, independence was granted to the second Boer republic, the Orange Free State.

The two Boer republics and the British were suspicious of each other's motives; Boers didn't trust the British and British high commissioners didn't want two large Boer nations on their northern border, since a significant number of Afrikaaners still lived in the colony in South Africa. Afrikaaner loyalty to Great Britain was by no means assured.

Diamonds were discovered in an area claimed jointly by the Transvaal, the Orange Free State and several of the indigenous native tribes. Fortune seekers, many of whom were English, poured into the area. Adding to the confusion, the miners, camp followers, and boomtown inhabitants set up their own pint-sized republic.

To bring some order to the situation, the British Government, in October 1871, took over the whole area as a British colony. This was, to the suspicious mind of the Boer, another example of the fact that no matter where they went, the British were always breathing down their necks.

Six years later, the British Government annexed the Transvaal. With their hands full fighting the Zulus, the ferocious black warrior nation that lived in the northeastern part of South Africa, the British had insufficient manpower to control their new recalcitrant subjects. The British administrator added insult to injury by treating the Boers like raw army recruits.

This heavy-handed treatment bore bitter fruit. On Christmas Day 1880 the Transvaal erupted in revolt. The First Boer War of liberation had begun. The British were so thoroughly defeated by the Boers that the government in London quickly granted them independence in 1881. It was not total freedom, however, since England retained authority over the Transvaal's foreign affairs; they remained involved in the actions of the Boer Republic.

Then, all too quickly, history repeated itself. In 1886, enormous amounts of gold were discovered in the heart of the Transvaal and gold-seeking foreigners poured in. The Republic was being overrun, and most important, every Boer tradition was being trod underfoot by the new arrivals.

In 1890, that grand imperial buccaneer Cecil Rhodes became Prime Minister of the British Cape Colony. Armed with this office, he resumed his dream of coloring the map of Africa British imperial red from the Cape to Cairo. Unfortunately, obstacles were close at hand—the two Boer republics, which Rhodes was determined to remove. With behind-the-scenes knowledge and tacit approval of the foreign office in London, Rhodes cooked up a flimsy excuse to invade the Transvaal. On December 29, 1985, Rhodes's scheme was born —the infamous Jameson Raid into the Transvaal to capture Johannesburg. The Raid was supposed to trigger a revolt by British residents of Johannesburg against the oppressive Boers. The affair was a disaster: poorly planned and executed, the revolt never started and Rhodes's band of pirates was easily and ignobly captured by the Boers.

Four years later, in October 1899, the last great assault of the 19th century against the Calvinist Afrikaaner culture was launched. The Boer War between the British Empire and the two Boer republics broke out. The British had manuevered the Boers into a war whose ramifications are still felt today. "I precipitated the crisis, which was inevitable, before it was too late," said the British High Commissioner to South Africa, Sir Alfred Milner. "It is not a very agreeable, and in many eyes, not very credible piece of business to have been largely instrumental in bringing about a big war."[2]

By 1902 the Boers were crushed, and imposed upon them was a system hostile to their cultural roots—British Crown Rule. Naturally, they feared for the very existence of their culture and traditions, as well they should have—the High Commissioner made it quite clear that he would pursue cultural genocide to destroy the Afrikaaner: "To knock the bottom out of the great Afrikaaner nation for ever and ever Amen."[3]

Milner's efforts were focused on the Boer's language. He was determined to rid the Boer Republic of its language by destroying its educational system—purging the Dutch infra-structure and replacing it with a British one. British teachers, principals and superintendents, appointed by British authorities in Cape Town, were given control of the Afrikaaner schools.

Like his predecessor Somerset in 1822, Milner imported teachers from England. The vast majority of them knew no Dutch and most didn't bother learning. Their mission, after all, was to supplant the Afrikaaner tongue with English. One can easily imagine the problems the scheme caused. A typical Afrikaaner reaction was, "We were taught by foreign teachers, by English teachers, all from England. We were an Afrikaans-speaking community, we'd hardly heard English spoken in our lives. The only English we had come in contact with was during the war and after the war."[4]

Not only was English the lingua franca in the classroom, but was required to be spoken on the playground during recess. If a child was caught speaking Afrikaans, he or she was forced to wear a placard around the neck stating, "I must not speak Dutch." Sometimes this punishment was reinforced by requiring the offending pupil to write on the blackboard, 1,000 times, "I must speak English at school." "Had it not been for Milner and his extreme measures," Kowie Marias, an opposition spokesman on education said, "we Afrikaaners would probably all quite happily have been speaking English by now. By his opposition to our language, he helped create it."[5]

Not all Afrikaans was completely outlawed in schools. Three hours of instruction in Afrikaans per week were permitted along with another two hours for religious instruction in the mother tongue. So the Afrikaaners had a choice: use the two hours designated for religious study to teach more Afrikaans, or study the Bible without a full knowledge of Afrikaans.

Milner explained his reasons for imposing the ban on Afrikaans to the Colonial Secretary in London: "The fact is, we are in this matter engaged in a fight with a very astute adversary [i.e., the Dutch Reformed Church] and there is no harm, in my opinion, in using the wisdom of the serpent against it."[6] Milner's policy facilitated the rise of private schools where young Afrikaaners could be taught by teachers chosen by the local community. However, to protect their community from subversion by the British, the Boers stepped outside their prior moral system and corrupted it. They formed clandestine organizations to protect their community by infiltrating the infrastructure of South Africa.

One of the most influential of these secret societies was the Broederbond, which was set up in 1918. At first, it was more of a fraternity whose aim was to create "an organization in which Afrikaaners could find each other and be able to work together for the survival of the Afrikaaner people in South Africa and the promotion of its [sic] interests."[7] However, members of the Broderbond who were teachers or civil servants claimed they were persecuted because of their open association with the society. As a result, in 1921 the members voted to turn the organization into a secret one and the Afrikaaner old boy network was born.

As the Broederbond grew, it increased the scope of its activities with the goal of preserving and advancing the language and culture of the Afrikaaner by utilizing this extensive network. In 1932, its chairman, professor J.C. Van Rooy of Potchfestroom University, told the members in a secret message: "After the cultural and economic needs, the Afrikaaner Broederbond will have to devote its attention to the political needs of our people. And here the aim must be a completely independent, genuine Afrikaaner government for South Africa. A government which, by its embodiment of our personal head of state, bone of our bone and flesh of our flesh, will inspire us and bind us together in irresistible unity and strength."[8]

Looking out for the political needs of the Afrikaaner (as perceived by the Broederbond) meant Afrikaaner support of the National Party led by D.F. Malan, whose aims coincided exactly with those of the Broederbond. They were soon working hand-in-glove. In 1948, Malan became the first National Party Prime Minister in South Africa. The Afrikaaner had taken absolute political control of South Africa and for the first time since the Union of South Africa was formed in 1910, every member of the Cabinet was an Afrikaaner. The Broederbond, founded to preserve Afrikaaner culture, had instituted one of its members as prime minister. Every prime minister since Malan has been a Broederbond member; thus began the Afrikaaner domination of South Africa.

Sadly, in this drive for power, the Afrikaaners abandoned their Calvinistic roots of individualism and clamped the collectivist social engineering policy of apartheid on South Africa—a far cry from the individual freedom enjoyed by their forefathers. They now resorted to the smoke-filled back-room tactics of a Tammany Hall political machine. They conspired in secret groups to subvert the efforts of British authorities. Their energies were directed toward preserving their culture with political power rather than with solutions based upon their moral framework of Biblical Calvinism. As a result, they became what they are today—a power-oriented socialistic society.

The Afrikaaners would deal with anyone if they thought it would further the Afrikaaner cause. In the 1930s and 40s, they dealt with labor unions to protect the rights of poor whites at the expense of Blacks and Coloreds. The result was the state-legislated policy of apartheid, which is essentially coming out of the smoke-filled rooms and going public with what had been planned in secret Broederbond meetings in the past.

A boost was given to the psyche of Afrikaanerdom as the process of anglicization that had been launched with such a vigor by Imperial Britain at the turn of the century was rolled back with a vengeance. Adopting an us versus them mentality, the Afrikaaners developed the policy of apartheid to preserve Afrikaanerdom from all perceived enemies, that is, anyone who is not Afrikaaner. The Afrikaaners swore they would never lose political control of the country again. They well remembered the British concentration camps that killed 26,000 Afrikaaners, mostly women and children.

Apartheid is directed at blacks for a simple reason. Although English-speaking South Africans were disliked by Afrikaaners, the latter grudgingly admitted that they were civilized people—white fellow Christians. For the Afrikaaner, the color white was equated with Christianity—civilized religion. The only difference between English whites and native blacks, as far as the Afrikaaner was concerned, was that the English were Christian—they were civilized, and therefore tolerable.

This is the priority for today's Afrikaaner as well as it was those of one hundred years ago. He is a strict Boer Calvinist first, a Protestant Christian second, a Western civilizationist third, a white "supremicist" fourth.

The 19th-century theological justification for the mid-20th-century political policy of apartheid is a view, as most South Africans realize, that is out of touch with the reality of the rapidly approaching 21st century. This mixing of theology and genetics gave South Africa its dangerous corrosive policy of apartheid. Its effect was so great that it severely damaged the relationship between the Afrikaaner and the Coloreds.

No population group in South Africa is closer to the Afrikaaner than those people of mixed blood called Coloreds. From the first days of the white settlers in South Africa in the mid-1600s, the Hottentots, the original natives encountered by white men, lived alongside the Boers, sharing their blood and learning their customs. They learned the Afrikaaner's language and contributed their own words and idioms. They worshipped together and lived as neighbors.

But apartheid, which was formed in the crucible of cultural war between the British and Afrikaaners, disenfranchised the Coloreds. They were taken off the voter lists and treated only slightly better than blacks. This turned the Colored against Afrikaaner policies.

While rolling back the British influence was important to the ego of the Afrikaaner, the corrupting side of the coin was devastating to his psyche. Now, thanks to apartheid, all relationships were determined socially instead of individually, as was the case for so much of their history. Biblical Calvinism, which had been their spiritual and moral foundation for long years, had been overpowered by secularism.

Secularism created a constant inner tension within the Afrikaaner over his historical sense of individualism (his classic Calvinist theological underpinnings) and the new doctrine of apartheid where relationships between the individuals were now determined by codified edicts of a bureaucratic socialized state.

This inner tension demonstrates the corruptiveness of apartheid because it was not in harmony with the basic moral principles of the people. Even though in the past individual Afrikaaners had treated non-whites very shabbily, it was not an institutionalized, state-mandated policy. Individuals could, and often did, treat non-whites more like fellow human beings. Under apartheid this option was no longer open to the individual.

Calvinism, the theological foundations of the Afrikaaner, is a very individualistic-centered theology and has deep roots within the Christian community in South Africa. Individual Afrikaaners are no more prone to racism than anyone else.

This is a key point to understand, for if (or rather when) apartheid is abolished, South Africa would not fall apart, as some maintain. Instead, it would regroup around the principles that more of them share—their Christian roots.

The prescription for constructive change, then, is a reaffirmation of traditional Calvinist beliefs. The Afrikaaners must rediscover their roots, so to speak. The Dutch

Reformed Church in South Africa, the keeper of the theological flame, has been corrupted by apartheid. Under apartheid, there are three main churches: one for the whites, one for the Coloreds and one for the blacks. The Gospel of Christ is preached along racial lines. In addition to its racial corruption, the Dutch Reformed Church has been preaching a 19th-century version of the Bible, which treats non-whites as heathens. Its theology does not seek a future kingdom of God on earth, which has contributed to their present dilemma because it led them to the idea that the covenant of God is essentially Afrikaans in nature—they, like the Old Testament Israelis, are the chosen people of God. This covenant with God theme permeates their theological, racial, cultural, historic, thinking because most important of all, they strongly believe it and further, believe it is permanently bound to them as received from their forefathers. Thus, Christian blacks cannot be Christian gentlemen, or Christian soldiers, or equals in the battle against atheistic communism creeping toward them under the direction of the Kremlin.

The Covenant of God theme—the theological foundation that permeates Afrikaaner thought—occurs throughout the Western world in communities strongly influenced by Calvinist Reformation. America's own period of Manifest Destiny is distinctly rooted in the same concepts. The process does not have to turn in on itself as it did in South Africa, but can expand and provide a forward-looking future vision of God's Kingdom on Earth as it its doing elsewhere in the Western World.

The same arguments Afrikaaners used to fashion apartheid were used by Calvinist thinkers in Geneva and Zurich, the intellectual centers of Calvinism during the Protestant Reformation, to fashion the Swiss Federation in the 17th century. South Africa has no more native antagonisms than those that formerly separated different linguistic, cultural and religious gorups in the Swiss Alps years ago. In fact, more than one scenario can be envisioned from the same Scriptural presuppositions. The present political and social gridlock is not a necessary consequence of Calvinism. This rethinking process has occurred in other Calvinistic communities. A re-analysis of basic Calvinist presuppositions has been suc-

cessful in Switzerland, Korea, the Netherlands and Nationalist China (Taiwan). The presence of South Africa's Colored
community is a graphic perpetual reminder that the current
Afrikaaner's forebears, steeped in Biblical Calvinism, once
held a very different interpretation of the Scriptural justification currently used to undergird apartheid's mandated separation of the races.

An intensely conservative people can often be led back to
ideas. Rather than circling the wagons and fighting to the
last Boer, the Afrikaaners can use their Calvinist roots to
guide them away from apartheid. Until recently, the Dutch
Reformed Church has failed to realize this, so the moral
vacuum has been filled by communists and the public nui-
sance, Bishop Tutu. As long as these groups occupy center
stage, chaos will reign and hope for reconciliation in South
Africa will fade.

The future of a peaceful South Africa depends on the
professors in the theology department of Stellenbosch University, the intellectual center of the Afrikaaner and foremost
bastion of apartheid. When the professors reconcile their
Calvinism with the moral and social reconstruction of South
Africa's government, then and only then will the Afrikaaner
have a reason to reach out and liberate the non-whites.

In fact, the Dutch Reformed Church is showing signs of
doing just that. The church's General Synod as recently as
1982 rejected all forms of racism "as being in conflict with
Scripture and as sin."[9] The influential Stellenbosch Presby-
tery declared: ". . . We admit that in the past the Dutch
Reformed Church has often lacked a clear Biblical vision for
the political and social life in our country. . . . In addition, we
urgently request that all discriminatory laws and regulations
be rescinded as soon as possible. . . ."[10]

Only when the Afrikaaner offers other South African
Christians the right hand of friendship will the wound-
healing process seriously begin.

1. Speech of Isaac Mokena to Faith America Foundation meeting in Washington D.C., January 28, 1986.

2. Thomas Pakenham, *The Boer War.* (New York: Random House, 1979), p. 116.

3. David Harrison, *The White Tribe of Africa: South Africa in Perspective* (Johannesburg: Macmillan S.A., 1983), p. 31.

4. Ibid., p. 53.

5. Ibid., p. 51.

6. Ibid., p. 52.

7. Ibid., p. 87

8. Ibid., p. 97.

9. Dr. James D. Colbert, "A Different View of South Africa," Christian Anti-Communist Crusade, Long Beach, Calif. (April 1986), p. 13.

10. Ibid., pp. 13-14.

15

Rolling Back The Mongols: A Good Dose of Capitalism

In many respects, South Africa is a sad country. Its unrealized economic potential could make it a Garden of Eden on the African continent, but government interference in the economy, official free enterprise rhetoric notwithstanding, has stifled the country's development.

The government owns coal-to-oil plants, the railroads, the telephone company and other major industries. Through licensing and regulations it controls all enterprise from banks to gold mines, from insurance companies to supermarkets. It even tells its citizens when they can buy toilet tissue, soap and dog food.

The heavy hand of government hurts all South Africans —black and white. Blacks are not allowed to open businesses in white areas; whites are not allowed to open businesses in black areas. Racist labor unions and other vested interests use government to enforce laws prohibiting whites from hiring blacks, barring them from competition in the labor market.

Yet, in spite of the governmental shackles on the South African economy, it remains the most vibrant on the continent. Like the United States, the South African economy functions in spite of, not because of, government interference.

"The solution to South Africa's problem," black economist Walter Williams said, "lies mostly in the creation of a state where there is freedom of human action—in a word, capitalism. Sadly enough, 'humanitarians' who say they want to help the blacks press for more socialism. They merely wish to change the color of the dictator."[1]

The rules and regulations of apartheid, which restrict blacks in their movement about the country and prohibit them from full enjoyment of the rights other South Africans enjoy, is a particularly obnoxious form of government regulation. Ironically, the left has saddled the right with apartheid (with the all-too-willing help of its friends in the media). But as the British historian Paul Johnson has pointed out, apartheid is ethnic socialism—it involves state interference throughout the entire economy to prohibit blacks from participating to the fullest extent possible. Apartheid has led to the creation of an enormous bureaucracy to oversee it; it takes an ever-growing slice of the national income and results in an endless proliferation of laws restricting the free market.

As Johnson said in his seminal article for *Commentary* magazine, "Capitalism and apartheid don't mix for broadly the same reason it cannot coexist with feudalism, or any other system which is based on inherited caste or race, or which forbids freedom of movement and the right of everyone to sell his or her labor where and when he or she chooses.

"It is the nature of capitalism in South Africa to destroy apartheid. It is under the pressure of capitalism, not the pressure of world opinion, that the government of P.W. Botha has been progressively dismantling the apartheid laws. There is a common interest for blacks and business to get rid of apartheid: for the former it is grotesquely unjust, for the latter it is grotesquely inefficient. This common interest is paradoxically emphasized by the disinvestment campaign, for if it succeeds, both will suffer."[2]

This fact may have dawned on the South African government of President P.W. Botha, who told his countrymen in an address in Durban on August 15, 1985: "I am of the opinion that there are too many rules and regulations in our country serving as stumbling blocks in the way of entrepreneurs.

"The underdeveloped part of the economy is mainly that of different non-white communities. Instead of the white [man] paternalistically trying to do everything for the Blacks, they must rather be allowed to help themselves. . . ."[3]

If South Africans follow this advice, it will open many doors for the black population. It is through a vibrant, expanding economy that the salvation of all South African blacks lies. This fact is recognized by blacks in South Africa who want real progress rather than recidivist violence. Mangosuthu G. Buthelezi, Chief of the Zulu nation, which numbers six to seven million and is the largest tribe in South Africa, said, "Without continued vibrant economic growth, without the kind of economic expansion attainable in the West, the future of Black South Africa is a bleak future if the struggle for liberation destroys our country's economic bases. The struggle for liberation will be in vain if it does no more than produce a change of government while at the same time creating an ungovernable situation."[4]

Like those of Williams and Johnson, Buthelezi's message is that capitalism, not more socialism or Marxist revolution, will liberate South African blacks. Blacks in South Africa are plagued by socialism and the cure for that plague is not more socialism. Not only would the destruction of South Africa's economy remove whatever chance there is for change for the better for blacks, it would drastically affect South Africa's neighbors to the north who depend so heavily on South African commerce. If the advocates of disinvestment are sincere in their call for a better life for South African blacks, then their toil is grossly misdirected. South African blacks do not need policies that will destroy the economic base of the country.

South Africa is faced with the dual problem of how to dismantle apartheid, with its myriad of petty, repressive, economic, social and other controls, and move toward a free society where all citizens are enfranchised with the same rights—those rights enjoyed by virtue of birth—without losing the support of the hardline constituency and without fueling revolutionary fire. Attempts at gradual, orderly reform have been met with cries that the regime is not doing enough, while at the same time, those efforts are construed as an admission of guilt for past crimes—as ratification of the program of the radicals.

A solution in South Africa that does not leave the African National Congress in power will not be satisfactory to the revolutionary left. Everyone from radical left Congressman Howard Wolpe (D-MI) to the pro-Soviet Randall Robinson calls for negotiations with "legitimate" black "leaders" such as the terrorist Nelson Mandela. Liberals believe that only violence will place blacks in a favorable position. ANC tactics reflect this and are moving the situation to a point where political accommodation and rapid reform will be nearly impossible.

Thus, the call for disinvestment. Outside investment in the South African economy has been the proximate cause for great strides made by blacks in South Africa. American investors, using the Sullivan principles, a suggested equal opportunity system for all employees of American firms in South Africa, has resulted in fair play in the work place, put blacks on the road to economic and political self-sufficiency. As long as blacks can move forward without the ANC, it and its communist cause is threatened. Investment in South Africa is a threat to those who favor violence because investment, which translates into economic power for blacks, which in turn can be parlayed into political power, would leave the ANC radicals out of the equation. Disinvestment will fuel the cause of the ANC and hurt the cause of freedom for black South Africans.

As Chief Buthelezi said, "Where, however, a people are suffering in desperate poverty and are struggling against inhuman odds, oppressed economically and economically fettered by Draconian laws supporting racist government, the question of strategies and tactics becomes crucial. The more desperate the situation the less room there is for making errors of judgment and the more tragic such errors of judgment become. No matter how human decency cries out against apartheid in the international community, no matter how repugnant apartheid appears to the world, and no matter how indignant the international community becomes about South Africa's internal policies, disinvestment is wrong strategy, a misguided strategy and a strategy which does not aid in the struggle for liberation at home."[5]

Most sensible South Africans, including high-level members of P.W. Botha's cabinet, realize and accept that blacks must play a greater part in South Africa's government. But they are solidly united in opinion that this progress must be an evolutionary rather than revolutionary change. Botha has made very clear that neither Soviet-backed, bomb-throwing terrorists nor their supporters in the West will set the agenda for change in South Africa: "We have never given in to outside demands and we are not going to do so. South Africa's problems will be solved by South Africans and not by foreigners. We are not going to be deterred from doing what we think best, nor will we be forced into doing what we do not want to do. The tragedy is that hostile pressure and agitation from abroad have acted as an encouragement to the militant revolutionaries in South Africa to continue their violence and intimidation. They have derived comfort and succor from this pressure.

"My government and I are determined to press ahead with our reform program, and to those who prefer revolution to reform, I say they will not succeed no matter how much support and encouragement they derive from outside sources. We can and we will resolve our problems by peaceful means. Despite the disturbances, despite the intimidation, there is more than enough goodwill among Blacks, Whites, Colored, and Asians to ensure that we shall jointly find solutions acceptable to us."[6]

Again, Buthelezi, the spokesman for the black majority and no political crony of Botha's, agreed: "It is a historical truism that every oppressed people have the responsibility of liberating themselves. Black South Africans have to conduct their own struggle to achieve their own victories and to establish a just, open and race-free society in their own land of birth. The liberation of South Africa cannot be achieved from without and it cannot be achieved by forces in the international community. Essentially apartheid must be defeated on the domestic front by people in the country, pursuing strategies and tactics which are most effective on the fronts where they struggle in their day to day lives. The defeat of apartheid must necessarily be achieved by a process of internal transformation and not by Black South Africans getting something for nothing. There will be no real victory unless it is a people's victory and unless the people's victory lays the foundation for a new society."[7]

This is not a message the ANC and their left-liberal supporters want to hear—especially from a black man. They want to hear Maxist rhetoric prompting young and old alike to violence. They want to transform South Africa into a socialist society. In short, the left does not want to free blacks —they want to enslave everyone. (And South Africans need only look north to see the grim future under conditions advocated by disinvestment backers and their Marxist-Leninist allies.)

The pace of reform of apartheid notwithstanding, it is unlikely that the South African government will succumb to ANC-inspired terror. Theodore Shackly, a covert-action expert, pointed out in the *The Journal of Defense and Diplomacy* that "South Africa has one of the 10 best armed forces in the world. As a result a decisive battle triggered by the ANC or any combination of southern Africans and Cubans is not a real-world scenario for the rest of this century."[8] A conventional invasion of South Africa by Soviet-backed forces of the front-line states is a very high-risk scenario to the would-be invader. Even in the 1960s when South Africa wasn't as powerful as it is now, according to a United Nations report it would "require 90,000 highly trained men with the most modern armaments, 700 aircraft and 100 ships and transports, all at astronomical cost."[9]

What hypocritical dogooders don't seem to realize is that their disinvestment-economic sanctions campaign is waging war upon the one institution that is most likely to destroy apartheid—capitalism. (On the other hand, maybe they do realize it and it is precisely for this reason they are so doggedly waging war on capitalism.)

South Africa, even with the limited amount of capitalism it practices produces a veritable feast of goods even though most (70 percent) of its land is either desert or mountains. Granted, South Africa and many of her impoverished neighbors have been blessed with natural resources. But in point of fact economic productivity is not dependent upon the presence of natural resources—look at prosperous Hong Kong, with no natural resources. Millions of very poor people in southern Africa have access to cultivable land, for example; their low productivity stems from primarily "want of ambition, energy and skill, and not want of land and capital."[10]

Peter Drucker points out that "no country is 'underdevel-

oped' because it lacks resources. 'Underdevelopment' is inability to obtain full performance from resources; indeed, we
should really be talking of countries of higher or lower
productivity rather than of 'developed' or 'undeveloped' countries. In particular, very few countries—Tibet and New Gui-
nea may be exceptions—lack capital. Developing countries
have, almost by definition, more capital than they productive-
ly employ."[11]

****

Capitalism cannot be thrust on every culture. It is
meaningless to continue saying, as do many observers, that
the Third World needs economic growth and capital investment. This is self-evident. The issue is why southern Africa,
Latin America, India—the undeveloped countries—resist
freedom and free enterprise. The answer is to be found in their
religious and cultural values.

Ludwig von Mises used India to demonstrate the problem: "India lacks capital because it never adopted the pro-
capitalist philosophy of the West and therefore did not remove
the traditional institutional obstacles to free enterprise and
big scale accumulation. Capitalism came to India as an alien
imported ideology that never took root in the minds of the
people."[12] Like apartheid in South Africa, there were and are
barriers in India, von Mises said, that prevented capitalism
from taking root. Indians imported into British colonies as
laborers took to capitalism like a duck takes to water. Some
are so successful in southern Africa they have been persecuted by the black leaders who took control when the British
relinquished control of its empire.

Even Britain itself was required to tear down barriers to
free enterprise before it became a world power. As described
by von Mises, "In the middle of the 18th century, conditions in
England were hardly more propitious than they are today in
India. The traditional system of production was not fit to
provide for the needs of an increasing population. The
number of people for whom there was no room left in the rigid
system of paternalism and governmental tutelage of business
grew rapidly. Although at that time England's population

was not much more than 15 percent of what it is today, there were several million of destitute poor. Neither the ruling aristocracy nor these paupers themselves had any idea about what could be done to improve the material conditions of the masses.

"The great change that within a few decades made England the world's wealthiest and most powerful nation was prepared for by a small group of philosophers and economists. They demolished entirely the pseudo-philosophy that hitherto had been instrumental in shaping the economic policies of the nation. . . . In short, these authors expounded the doctrine of free trade and laissez-faire. They paved the way for a policy that no longer obstructed the businessman's effort to improve and expand his operations.

"What begot modern industrialization and the unprecedented improvement in material conditions that it brought about was neither capital previously accumulated nor previously assembled technological knowledge. In England, as well as in other Western countries that followed it on the path of captialism, the early pioneers of capitalism started with scanty capital and scanty technological experience. At the outset of industrialization was the philosophy of private enterprise and initiative, and the practical application of this ideology made the capital swell and the technological know-how advance and ripen."[13]

This means that fundamental ideological and political change must occur in South Africa and her neighbors if the region is ever to reach its economic potential. It means scrapping the murderous doctrine of socialism, in whatever form, be it South Africa's apartheid or Tanzania's variety, combined with vigorous new business investment in countries friendly to the United States.

When and if this day comes, it will be important to remind all South Africans that even a free market requires a moral foundation. As pointed out by the economist Wilhelm Ropke, "It should not be forgotten that the 'economic man' of the classics was really an English gentlemen of the 18th century, whose Norman code was fixed by the church and by tradition. In fact, the market economy is an economic system which cannot exist without a minimum of mutual trust, confidence

168 RED STAR OVER SOUTHERN AFRICA

in the stability of the legal-institutional framework of the economic process (including money), contractual loyalty, honesty, fair play, professional honor, and that pride which considers it beneath one to cheat, bribe or misuse the authority of the state for one's own egotistic purpose. Above all, there must be a 'creed' in the most general sense of the term, a belief in a definite scale of ultimate values giving sense and purpose to the ordinary doings of all participating in the economic process, and finally, at least a provisional understanding of the meaning and working of this economic process."[14]

South Africa needs a good dose of capitalism.

1. Walter Williams, "Socialism Plagues South Africa," *Richmond Times-Disptach* (February 26, 1984).
2. Paul Johnson, "Sanctions and Their Ramifications," *The Sunday Star* (London, February 9, 1986).
3. Address by P.W. Botha at the opening of the National Party Natal Congress in Durban on August 15, 1985.
4. Statement of M.G. Buthelezi, Chief Minister, Kwazulu, in Ulandi on March 9, 1984.
5. Ibid.
6. Botha, op. cit.
7. Buthelezi, op. cit.
8. Theodore G. Shackley, "South Africa: The Circle of Insurgency," *Journal of Defense and Diplomacy* (November 19&5), p. 53.
9. Paul L. Moorcraft, *Africa's Super Power* (Johannesburg: Sygma/Collins, 1981), p. 186.
10. P.T. Bauer, *Reality and Rhetoric: Studies in the Economics of Development* (Cambridge, Mass.: Harvard University Press, 1984), p. 8.
11. Peter F. Drucker, *Towards the Next Economics* (New York: Harper & Row, 1981), p. 65.
12. Ludwig von Mises, *Planning for Freedom*, 4th ed. (South Holland, Ill.: Libertarian Press, 1980), p. 202.
13. von Mises, 200 ff.
14. Wilhelm Ropke, *International Economic Disintegration* (London: Hodge [1942], 1950), pp. 68-69.

16

Trouble In Marxist Paradise

The facade of communist invulnerability is beginning to crack. Until recently, policy makers and intellectuals in both the East and West took as gospel the notion that once the beast of Marxist-Leninist communism had fixed its evil grip upon an unfortunate people, they were doomed to perpetual enslavement. Unfortunately, many policymakers and intellectuals still believe the myth of communist invincibility.

The sanitized term in use in the mundane spheres of diplomacy and editorial comment is the "Brezhnev Doctrine." This postulated the guarantee that communism was a sure winner. When a communist imperialistic war of imposition, not liberation, succeeded, it would be irreversible.

With the West quaking in its boots after the United States pulled out of Vietnam, nation after nation fell under the jack-boot of Soviet imperialism: Ethiopia in 1974, Vietnam in 1975, followed quickly by Cambodia, Mozambique and Angola. Then, near the end of the 70s Nicaragua and Afghanistan felt the sting of Marxist imperialism.

The Brezhnev Doctrine was a global reality.

Showing the conviction of cowards, the U.S. State Department and its intellectual apologists chimed in with the American answer to Brezhnev's challenge. In 1976, Helmut Sonnenfeldt, a protege of Henry Kissinger, formulated America's counter doctrine which stated that the West's interests are best served if the Soviet Union enjoys undisturbed the fruits of conquest. In other words, the Sonnenfeldt doctrine condemned millions to perpetual slavery.

Fortunately, not all people in the world acquiesced to Soviet domination. In countries such as Angola and Mozambique, the people struggled long and hard to free themselves from colonial rule. Unfortunately, their struggles were be-

Government controlled areas are limited to near urban areas. Renamo controls 85% of Mozambique.

Jonas Savimbi: Leader of the anti-communist UNITA freedom fighters in Angola

UNITA officials at their headquarters in Jamba: (from L to R): Chief of Staff, Chiliteguna; UNITA Permanent Secretary, Puna; and Foreign Minister, Chingunji

UNITA soldiers prepare to move out of Jamba.

UNITA gunsmiths repair damaged assault rifles.

UNITA has its own shops where they repair captured weapons. If necessary, they can build some of their own weapons. Here a UNITA blacksmith prepares to repair a truck spring.

Alfonso Dklakama, head of RENAMO

RENAMO freedom fighters on patrol looking for the Marxist enemy.

RENAMO freedom fighters relax after capturing a town formerly held by the Marxist regime.

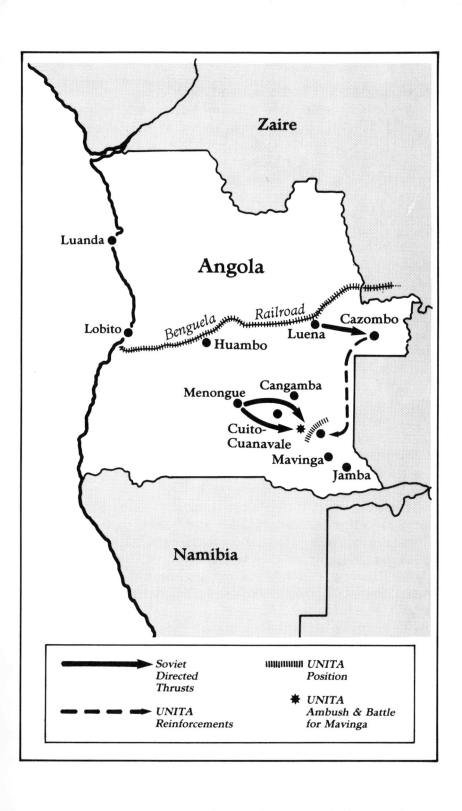

trayed and these countries found themselves victimized by a more vicious, determined colonial power, the Soviet Union. The old colonial yoke had been tossed off only to be replaced by the shackles and chains of Soviet tyranny.

Unlike the West, infected by what Solzhenitsyn calls "the western disease," the people in Angola and Mozambique are made of sterner stuff. In these countries, the people, although tired and weary from years of war, once again became soldiers, as their nations again became battlefields in the effort to become free. (This phenomenon is not limited to southern Africa. Today the people of Afghanistan, Cambodia, Laos, Vietnam and Ethiopia are also waging wars of true liberation against Soviet colonialism.)

For almost a decade, wars of liberation have been fought against Soviet-style, Marxist-Leninist regimes on opposite coasts of southern Africa—Angola, on the Atlantic Ocean, and Mozambique, on the Indian Ocean.

Let us now take a closer look at these two movements, with the major emphasis on Angola, for the simple reason that more information is available on the struggle in Angola (for reasons that will become clearer later on) than that in Mozambique.

Early in 1976, after UNITA's defeat in the Angola civil war, Jonas Savimbi was forced to lead his loyal supporters on a gruelling long march deep into the country's interior, pursued by the victorious MPLA and their Cuban mercenary allies. Pursuit was so tenacious that Savimbi and his harried followers dared not sleep in the same place for more than two nights in a row. Savimbi started his Long March with 3,000 men; it ended with 67. More than 800 died; the rest left him or faded away into the bush.

Deep in the wilds of Angola's southeasternmost province, Cuando Cubango, called by the Portuguese "the Land at the End of the World," Savimbi halted and began rebuilding his guerrilla force. As the movement developed Savimbi followed five principles in carrying out his war of liberation against the communist dictatorship in Luanda. They were:

1) The guerrillas must be in a symbiotic relationship with the people, whose support, overt and covert, was essential to any success we could achieve.

2) The movement must have a clearly defined political program and objective. UNITA's program was simple and clear: it fought for an independent Angola, free of all foreign troops. It believed that the individual, not the state, should own farmland. UNITA advocated free democratic elections, freedom of religion, and respect for tribal customs and languages.

3) Unity of purpose was Savimbi's third key point. His guerrillas could win only if their military and political efforts were all working in the same direction. Any lack of coordination in the efforts could only hurt the guerrilla's cause.

4) It was essential that the guerrilla base of operations be within the territory of its own nation. His movement would not be conducted from the glittery jet-set atmosphere of European capitals, as were the Marxist-dominated guerrilla movements of SWAPO or the ANC. Savimbi's sanctuary, so vital to any guerrilla movement, would be in Angola.

5) UNITA would establish international ties. It would seek allies throughout the world who would give it military, political and propaganda support. As a result, UNITA has representatives in Washington, London, Paris, Munich, Geneva, Portugal, Morocco and Senegal. For this reason more is known about Angola's struggle to rid itself of Soviet domination than about Mozambique's similar war of liberation. (This is changing, however, as the Mozambican resistance group is in the process of establishing its representatives in the West.)

During the early years of rebuilding, Savimbi's tactics followed classic rules of guerrilla warfare. When confronted by a superior enemy, the guerrillas carefully avoided any conventional, set-piece confrontation with the MPLA and their Cuban Praetorian Guards. This was not out of a reluctance to fight, but simply due to the fact that Savimbi's men lacked the manpower and firepower to go head-to-head with the Cubans and MPLA.

Instead, UNITA concentrated on ambushes, sabotage (particularly of the Benguela railroad, eventually rendering it inoperable), mine-laying, long-distance mortar bombardment, etc. Their tactics of the moment were designed to harass their enemy, disperse already thinly-stretched MPLA forces, cut lines of communication and confine the bulk of the enemy's forces to defending major towns and strategic centers. They were largely successful in this task.

Meanwhile, UNITA was improving its hold on the rural areas under its control and winning the hearts and minds of the population there. The time between 1981 and 1986 was a period of retrenchment, consolidation, recruitment and training of the UNITA guerrillas. The imposition of Soviet-style totalitarian oppression by the MPLA on the Angolan people caused a flood of refugees and recruits to UNITA's cause.

By 1981 UNITA had become strong enough to begin moving out of its remote areas and to take the fight to the MPLA. Soon the guerrilla movement had acquired total control over huge amounts of land in southeastern and eastern Angola, as well as in the vitally important central highlands. As a result of this expansion of influence and control, the MPLA and Cuban forces in these areas are currently restricted to the major garrison towns and depend mainly on re-supply by air.

In rural areas under its control, UNITA established permanent operational and training bases in addition to safe supply routes to the various military fronts where they are now operating. By acquiring and establishing these safe base areas, UNITA was ready for an intensified military campaign to oust the MPLA regime, rather than having to rely on scattered guerilla attacks.

Beginning in 1982, thanks to the formation of newly-established, semi-regular units and better equipment, UNITA went on the offensive. Savimbi thought his forces strong enough to attack the MPLA's strong points, heavily defended positions and even large towns, which, until then, they had prudently avoided. Previously, UNITA would abandon captured villages or towns in the face of the inevitable MPLA/Cuban counterattack. Now Savimbi's men didn't fade away but followed the concept of "capture-and-hold." The results of UNITA's new offensive strategy, although it has been modified to cope with the recent Soviet-directed attempt to crush Savimbi, were spectacular. Key towns fell to Savimbi's troops and UNITA extended its control and influence over a wider area of Angola.

His organized efforts and the training given his troops began to bear fruit, as Savimbi committed his forces to conventional battles. Mavinga, the second largest town in Cuando Cubango province, felt Savimbi's sting. Guarded by a brigade of 2,000 MPLA soldiers, the town was attacked by UNITA on September 19, 1980. After a fierce battle lasting only four hours, the MPLA fled Mavinga, suffering casualties approaching 50 percent and abandoning huge stores of arms, ammunition and equipment that were quickly added to UNITA's arsenal. Interestingly enough, there were significant reinforcements available to the communist defenders of Mavinga—6,000 Cuban and MPLA troops at Menongue and 4,000 at Cuito Cuanavale—but they refused to help their beleaguered comrades at Mavinga. Six months later, in March 1981, the MPLA launched a major effort to recapture the town from UNITA. The attempt failed when UNITA ambushed the relief column some 70 kilometers west of Mavinga and destroyed it, killing some 800 MPLA troops in the process.

Although Mavinga was UNITA's most successful victory between 1980-1981, Savimbi's forces didn't rest on their laurels. They launched other actions that proved they had moved from guerrilla warfare into the conventional war stage. They demonstrated skill in command, logistics, communications, and carried out with imagination and success tactical engagements that led to the defeat of forces possessing superior equipment and air support.

It was a force that the Soviets and MPLA could no longer ignore. By the end of 1981, UNITA had 15,000 freedom fighters operating in groups of 30 to 150 in every province in southern Angola, and had trained and equipped 10 to 15 conventional combat battalions. It claimed to hold most of the provinces of Moxico and Cuando Cubango and half of Cuenne. Under its control were 2.5 million Angolans. By the start of 1983, UNITA had doubled the area under its control as a result of a series of fierce battles fought during the previous six months. The fall of Gago Coutinho gave UNITA control of most of the eastern Angolan border with Zambia. As a result, a line of smaller towns quickly fell to UNITA, which pushed its forces to within 32 kilometers of Luena, a major MPLA/

Cuban-held town on the Benguela railroad.

One of UNITA's main strategic goals in 1983 was to open a corridor from its territory in the southeast to the center of Angola in order to establish a secure supply route to its forces operating in central Angola. This was accomplished and UNITA operations continued to expand: The province of Cuanza Norte, Malanje, and southern Luanda, to within 200 kilometers of Luanda, Angola's capital, felt the presence of UNITA's forces, which also began operations in the northern province of Uige, home of the Bakongo tribesmen, the tribal base of Holden Roberto's moribund FNLA resistance movement.

In the fall of 1983, UNITA claimed control of the entire region south of the Benguela railroad from the Zaire-Zambia border to the Cuito-Menongue road, a territory encompassing some 150,000 square miles. Only the town of Cuito Cuanavale remained in MPLA hands, though it had to be re-supplied by air. Nevertheless, this town would become an important stage in future MPLA operations against Savimbi.

In addition, UNITA's northern commander had moved his forces to positions where they overran the major town of Caculo on the main tarred road from Luanda to Lunda. At least 10 battalions, each with 600-800 men, were operating north of the Benguela railroad. In two areas, UNITA regulars were operating at brigade strength of almost 3,000 men. In addition, in action hundreds of kilometers in front of these regular forces, groups of UNITA guerrillas, ranging in size from 15 to 200 men, were planting mines, blowing up bridges, ambushing convoys, attacking small outposts and hitting such economic targets as power stations and dams. As a result of these campaigns of 1982 and 1983, UNITA has expanded either its territory or area of operations by hundreds of kilometers, carrying the war to the enemy and transferring the focus from operations in the south to the north.

A first-hand account of the dramatic reversal of the situation in Angola was provided by the British journalist Fred Bridgland who, after spending several weeks with Savimbi's forces near the end of 1983, reported that "it is difficult to convey adequately how total and sophisticated is the degree of UNITA military control, now extending to more than a third of the country. Military bases, logistic bases, state farms, schools, hospitals, and civilian villages under UNITA control are scattered throughout the area. Hundreds of trucks ply up and down the Savimbi trail carrying supplies right into the centre of Angola. Rebel trucks move freely for many hundreds of kilometers through Angola without any fear of running into enemy mines or ambushes."[1]

UNITA's recent tactics have included infiltrating major cities like Huambo and Luanda with commando units trained for urban sabotage. On April 21, 1984, one of these units exploded a bomb at the Soviet-Cuban headquarters in Huambo. A large number of Soviet and Cuban officers were killed by the blast. Another result was the explosion of simmering tensions between the Angolans and Cubans, culminating in a three-hour gun battle between the MPLA and the Cubans, which occurred in the wake of the Huambo bomb blast. The battle only ceased with the personal intervention of the provincial governor.

The morale of the Angolan Army (FAPLA) is plumeting due to a number of factors, one of which is the general misery that exists, throughout Marxist totalitarian states. FAPLA uses forced conscription to get its soldiers. This, coupled with the poor quality of the training they receive (the Marxist guerrillas, SWAPO, get better training at their bases in Angola than that given to the Angolan Army) makes FAPLA a less than efficient fighting force. As one can imagine, under these circumstances there is no great rush by Angolan youths to flock to the colors to defend the misery, shortages, abuse and deprivation that is endemic to a Marxist society. It is no wonder that the MPLA regime has had to increase its armed manpower by forced conscription.

The preferential treatment given the Cubans, Russians, and Eastern bloc personnel by the Angolan government in the matter of food, fuel, supplies, etc., doesn't enhance FAPLA's morale either. Nor does the reluctance of the Cubans to leave the relative safety of the major towns and fight UNITA in the bush prompt solidarity among the Marxist allies. Many FAPLA soldiers vote with their feet and desert to the UNITA cause.

This plummeting morale has affected the performance of the Angolan Army on the battlefield. Fred Bridgland vividly illustrates this in his account of the battle for Alto Chicapa on November 29, 1983: "I suspect the battle for Alto Chicapa was over before it began. The garrison had no grain and was down to its last few tins of pork luncheon meat. . . . There was no electricity. The power station generator was in working order, but there was no diesel fuel to drive it. There was no running water because of the lack of electricity to pump water from the river to the town reservoir. Toilets in the barracks and in the gracious stucco colonial houses, occupied by officers, were hideously blocked. The only transport possessed by the garrison were two trucks without wheels. . . .

"One prisoner, a Sergeant Andre, commander of a platoon of 50 men, said three of his soldiers and 120 from the garrison as a whole had deserted. They were leaving because of hunger. It is three months since trucks last reached us with supplies. In many cases we were having to survive by stealing. . . . We weren't supplied regularly with food because we had no Cubans or East Germans with us."[2]

The deteriorating military situation has alarmed the Soviet colonial masters in Angola. They drastically stepped up their military aid to the puppet government in Luanda. A partial list of Soviet aid to Angola gives a picture of the murderous intent of the communists: 25 armored cars, 34 57mm anti-aircraft guns, 100 other AA guns, 96 T-34 tanks, 34 T-54 tanks, 3 T-62 tanks, 46 personnel carriers (BTR-60), 140 cargo trucks, 211 other military vehicles, 30 MIG-21e (Fishbed), 40 MI HIND helicopter gunships, and 160,000 tons of small arms and ammunition.[3] The Soviets determined to crush UNITA once and for all.

During August 1985 the communists launched a major dry season offensive using massive airpower, tanks, and 20,000 troops under the control of Russian General Konstantin Chaknovich. The Soviets were in this offensive up to their eyeballs, exercising tactical control of the communist forces down to the battalion level. The ultimate objective of the offensive was to capture Jamba, UNITA's capital, and the destruction of Savimbi and his movement.

The Soviets knew that UNITA lacked air defense and

anti-tank weapons and they thought their armor and air power would carry the day, but they miscalculated the fighting ability of the UNITA forces and the military skill of Savimbi and his officers. UNITA troops skillfully withdrew their forces in the face of the massive armor thrust, luring the armored columns deep into the bush where Savimbi's forces could attack them on their flanks.

The battle plan of the Soviets called for launching a two-front offensive on August 15—one from the towns of Luena and Moxico. The Soviet-directed column from these towns, using Russian T-34, T-55 and new model T-62 tanks, would move east into the Cazombo salient that juts into neighboring Zambia, capture the town of Cazombo, then turn southward and link up with the second offensive column. This thrust was a feint. The true mission of the offensive was tasked to the second offensive column, which was to move southeast from Menongue to Cuito Cuanavle. There it would split into two prongs and initiate a pincer movement attack upon its objective—Mavinga. From Mavinga the communist forces would pose a direct threat to Savimbi's headquarters and stronghold in Jamba.

That was the plan. Executing it proved to be another matter, as UNITA was determined to stop it. "If we don't survive, we die," Savimbi said. "I am bound to survive."[4]

The two pincers ran into difficulties. The right flank, caught in the soft sandy soil, was attacked by several UNITA brigades. The other flank was called upon for assistance. As the left flank moved to help, it was raked by UNITA mortar and artillery fire. The huge armored vehicles and trucks of the column couldn't manuever in the soft, sandy tracks and were destroyed en masse. Savimbi, seeing the plight of the MPLA columns, showed his brilliant generalship: He ordered most of his soldiers defending Cazombo from the northern column to reinforce the defenders of Mavinga. These moved rapidly over 200 kilometers and enabled Savimbi to concentrate his forces while the MPLA forces were divided. UNITA launched a counterattack on September 26 and after three days of heavy fighting, the Soviet-directed troops withdrew.

The battle at Mavinga was a major victory for UNITA, inflicting severe casualties on the communist forces, including 2,300 men killed, 79 vehicles destroyed, 52 captured, and 22 aircraft, including at least one MIG-21, shot down.

The northern communist MPLA column had a bit more success. On September 29 it attacked Cazombo, denuded of UNITA troops which had been pulled out to help Savimbi at Mavinga, and forced UNITA to withdraw from Cazombo. The capture of Cazombo was little more than a Pyrrhic victory for the MPLA since UNITA still controls the surrounding area around Cazombo and it can only be re-supplied by air.

The 1985 Soviet-directed offensive by the MPLA was the strongest challenge to UNITA since the MPLA seized power in Angola a decade ago. It clearly indicates that the MPLA is not going to be "weaned" away from the Soviets by the soothing words of naive diplomats at the State Department. Instead, the Soviets are launching a war of attrition against UNITA, using conventional Warsaw Pact-style tactics— massive armored attacks supported by air power. Although UNITA has received U.S. Stinger anti-aircraft missiles and a commitment from President Reagan for $15 million in American aid, it still lacks credible anti-tank weaponry and may be forced to abandon its semi-conventional warfare and go back to a purely guerrilla campaign.

It is clear that the Savimbi's bush war against the Soviet colonizers in Angola is far from over.

****

Mozambique

Meanwhile, on the opposite coast of Africa, another anti-communist insurgency is being waged in Mozambique.

The Marxist terrorist group FRELIMO had been handed power in Mozambique on a platter after the leftist coup in Lisbon. But FRELIMO was totally unprepared when, over-night, it was faced with the responsibility of running the country. It was not up to the task.

Machel's communists conducted a campaign of terror and expropriation against both the black and white middle class in Mozambique. As a result, ninety percent of the

Portuguese settlers left the country and took their finances and expertise with them, leaving Mozambique to the tender mercies of the Marxists. The brain drain caused by the exodus of the Portuguese and the imposition of socialism had predictable results—the erosion of individual freedom and a ruined economy.

This didn't endear FRELIMO to the vast majority of the Mozambicans. Under Machel's communist reign, Mozambique became one of the world's poorest nations, officially listed as an underdeveloped country by the United Nations. Yet in spite of the intense hatred for FRELIMO, at that stage few Mozambicans were willing to take up arms against their new masters. But this situation was soon to change.

The Rhodesians had been very concerned with events unfolding in their neighbor to the east. With the ascension to power of Machel's communists and the closing of Mozambique's borders with Rhodesia, the Rhodesians faced serious logistic problems: They had lost their links to Mozambique's east coast ports and thus a outlet for a high percentage of their exports. In addition, Rhodesia now had another enemy on her eastern border that posed an expanded military threat to the Rhodesians. The problem facing Rhodesia was whether it could sit back and allow Machel to export violence and terrorism. Something had to be done to counter this threat with the limited resources and manpower available to the Rhodesians.

The method chosen in 1976 was simple: take advantage of the strong anti-FRELIMO feeling that already existed in Mozambique and start a black resistance movement that could wage guerrilla war against the communist government. So Rhodesia, fighting against its own guerilla resistance, was organizing and encouraging an organization with a similar motive in Mozambique. Unfortunately, the mission was faced with immediate problems, chiefly a lack of money. To add insult to injury, no weapons were provided with which to arm any guerrillas that might be organized.

Despite these shortcomings, the Rhodesians made the best of a bad situation. They spent most of 1976 studying the mood among Mozambicans in the border area. What they discovered was encouraging. As a result of Machel's marxification of the country, there was indeed an intense hatred against FRELIMO. How to transform this hatred into a rebel army without having any funds or weapons became the problem for the Rhodesians to overcome. Since they had no money or weapons, the Rhodesians decided to wage a war of words using as ammunition the power of the pen and FRELIMO's poor track record.

To intensify the hatred and discontent with FRELIMO and get word of the new Mozambique National Resistance Movement (RENAMO) to the common man in Mozambique, a clandestine radio station, The Voice of Free Africa, was established. Located in Gwelo, inside Rhodesia, the station began broadcasting in June 1976 using a 400 kilowatt transmitter. The Voice monitored Mozambique's news commentaries, quickly rewrote them to support RENAMO, and rebroadcast their own communiques back into Mozambique.

The results were immediate and encouraging, but embarrassing to the Rhodesians since they were faced with countless FRELIMO soldiers deserting to join the resistance but unable to find it since it existed in name only. It became obvious that the campaign was working and that the nonexistent rebel army would have no problem recruiting soldiers. But unless the would-be rebels were organized, trained and given weapons, the support would soon evaporate.

Through the efforts of wealthy retornados (Portuguese Mozambicans who had fled to Portugal) and some Middle Eastern countries sold on the concept of a pro-Western Mozambican resistance movement, financing was secured to buy arms and start training the recruits who had shown up looking for RENAMO. A secret training camp was set up at an isolated farm at Odzi, close to Umtali, near the Mozambican border. But one vital igredient was still missing. The new rebel army had no leader, which is a must in a guerrilla movement.

Then one day the Rhodesians' prayers were answered. A former FRELIMO platoon commander, Andre Matsangaidze, escaped from a FRELIMO re-education camp and made his way across the border to Umatali. He had heard about the resistance movement and was eager to join. He had an ax to grind and was anxious to settle old scores. Matsangaidze was a charismatic, fearless leader who assured the Rhodesians that attracting disgruntled FRELIMO to the ranks of the resistance movement would be easy. A deal was struck—if he could get the men, the Rhodesians would make him the leader of the RENAMO resistance movement. To make sure Matsangaidze was the correct choice, the Rhodesians decided to test him. His first task was to go back into Mozambique with a small group of guerrillas, attack his old re-education camp at Gorongoza and release the prisoners. It was a demanding task but Matsangaidze was equal to it. Early in 1977, leading his small band of men, they mounted a successful attack that freed 500 prisoners from the camp. The Mozambique National Resistance movement had the right man to lead it!

Three hundred of the freed men decided to cast their lot with Matsangaidze and set off for Rhodesia. For good measure, they wreaked havoc along the way by stealing equipment and shooting at any FRELIMO that crossed their path en route back to the border. By means of daring attacks Matsangaidze was able to recruit an ever-growing number of escapees from Machel's prison camps and disgruntled FRELIMO soldiers deserting the Marxist cause to join the resistance movement.

In mid 1978 Mozambique's second war of liberation began. RENAMO conducted raids and ambushes on FRELIMO garrisons and convoys and targeted the transportation infrastructure at key points such as bridges. The resistance gathered strength and momentum, with the response to recruiting so overwhelming that it became difficult to keep up with it. Potential recruits often had to be turned away. Even today, RENAMO has more men than it has arms to give them!

Soon the Marxist government of Machel was faced with the same bush warfare tactics it had used in the past when fighting the Portuguese. The chickens were coming home to roost.

In January 1979 the resistance got a big shot in the arm when the Rhodesian Army's elite Special Air Service (SAS) began operating with them. The SAS could draw upon years of unique experience that eager pupils in the resistance movement were only too happy to learn. SAS elements accompanied Matsangaidze and 200 of his men when RENA-MO established its main permanent base in the Gorongoza mountains of Sofala province. Gorongoza was a perfect guerrilla hideout, with meadows, valleys, clear streams of water, a fringe of forest, all more than a mile above the lowlands. It had excellent concealment and overhead cover from spotter planes, yet it provided a view of all the major roads and surrounding countryside.

One of the SAS's first jobs was to help RENAMO build a permanent base camp in its mountain headquarters. They helped RENAMO site its defenses, build a rifle range and select access tracks. Later, groups of SAS teams would build hospitals and underground depots for ammunition, and reorganize the stores and teach hygiene and communications skills.

They improved shooting skills with AK-47 assault rifles —the true weapon of revolution—and the equally-favored and deadly RPG-7 rocket launcher. They taught the rebels how to be devious guerrillas, how to derail trains, showed them the best places to lay ambushes and landmines, and how to do it quickly. The Rhodesians, of necessity masters at improvisation, taught RENAMO how to salvage whatever could be useful to its cause. For example, how the bits and pieces of old weapons lying around their bases could be made into working weapons.

From the start of its guerrilla war against FRELIMO, RENAMO spent a lot of time and energy to win the hearts and minds of the Mozambican masses. The message was one of Mozambican nationalism instead of trading one colonial master—the Portuguese—for a far worse one—the Soviets; defending and respecting the traditions of the various Mozambican cultures and religions versus Marxist dictatorship; and freedom and the right of every Mozambican to earn his living as he saw fit, instead of the forced slavery of communism.

Initially, as the guerrillas had no other means of supply, every patrol staggered into the bush weighed down with salt, food and seeds to give the villagers. Salt was worth its weight in gold and often paid the way into an area. After the permanent base was established at Gorongoza, the seeds and salt were flown in, enabling the guerrillas to grow their own goods and become self-sufficent.

The locals welcomed RENAMO wherever it went and the ranks of the resistance movement swelled. The Voice of Free Africa was broadcasting its message to good effect. RENAMO'S long string of successes—which were confirmed by intercepts monitored by sophisticated equipment—were broadcast throughout Mozambique. Everything was going well.

Then on October 17, 1979, disaster struck when, leading an attack in Gorongoza town, Andre Matsangaidze was killed. The loss of RENAMO's foolhardy but brave leader was devastating. After a brief power struggle, Matsangaidze's deputy Alfonso Dhlakama assumed control

In spite of the death of its leader and the brief upheaval over Dklakama's assumption of command, RENAMO continued operations and as time moved on, gained new ground and became accepted by a vast portion of the population as a viable opposition to the Machel government. Every successful ambush produced more captured weapons, food and experience.

When RENAMO first began its campaign to topple Machel, Radio Maputo referred to the rebels as "bandits." By 1979, they had changed their tune and were calling them "the enemy." But change was in the air, as soon, through the duplicitous efforts of the British, Robert Mugabe would take the reins of power in Zimbabwe, the new name for Rhodesia, and the Rhodesian help would end, since Mugabe and Machel were Marxist allies

RENAMO would need a new sanctuary when Mugabe took power. There was only one alternative outside of giving up the fight, and that was to get help from the South Africans. For a black African leading a fight to free his country from a Marxist tyranny, this was a tough thing to do. Yet, what alternative did RENAMO have? The country that has carried the beacon of individual freedom in the world—the United States—was too busy accommodating the Soviets to hold out a helping hand for the people struggling to throw off the yoke of tyranny.

The South Africans, not overjoyed at the prospect of

being surrounded by hostile Marixist states, were glad to assist RENAMO. Shortly before Mugabe took power, RENAMO pulled out of Rhodesia and set up shop in South Africa at Phlalborwa near the Mozambique border. A training base was set up and the Voice of Free Africa went back on the air, beaming its broadcasts into Mozambique. Regular air drops were organized, bringing medical supplies and captured Soviet-bloc arms to RENAMO's bases inside Mozambique.

RENAMO went back to waging guerrilla war against the Marxist government. Its targets were Mozambique's economy, its infrastructure and Samora Machel's government. Prime targets were rail lines, power lines, roads, bridges, and the oil pipeline from Beira to Mutare in Zimbabwe.

RENAMO's actions bore fruit as its area of control greatly expanded. It now operates in every province in Mozambique controlling 85% of the country and threatens the capital of Maputo, which is under seige.

A British intelligence report of September 1984 stated that FRELIMO had lost most of Mozambique north of the Save River (three-fourths of the country). Peasants in Tete province, for example, were "almost irretrievably disillusioned with FRELIMO, having turned to arms in much the same way their fathers became FRELIMO fighters against colonial rule."[5]

As a result, FRELIMO stays in its garrisons and only ventures out to the countryside in large, well-armed convoys. Morale within FRELIMO is plummeting and its ranks are riddled with RENAMO informers and sympathizers. It has gotten so bad for FRELIMO that a recent British intelligence estimate reported that "many MNR commanders are former FRELIMO cadres who still have well-placed friends in FRELIMO. The MNR consistently obtains information about personnel, arms and food movements throughout the country. The ambush and sabotage success rate is high."[6]

RENAMO's former Secretary General, Evo Fernandes, confirmed the sorry state of FRELIMO's armed forces: ". . . the real problem in this war—in any war—is the problem of moral capacity, the willingness to fight your enemy to win. We have it. They are losing it. This is the real situation. If the FRELIMO armed forces were professional armed forces, then they would have their own quarters, shops, cinemas and so on. They would live outside the civilian society. But the army is a conscripted one. All the problems in the civilian society are reflected in the army. If there is no food, no transport, then the people do not want to fight. We are fighting in all the provinces of Mozambique. It was like a flood from the middle of 1982 onwards."[7]

RENAMO's success caused the Marxist regime of Samora Machel to turn to his hated enemies for help—the capitalist West and the Republic of South Africa. Machel turned to the South Africans with the self-serving proposition that if South Africa would cease aiding RENAMO, Machel would boot the African National Congress (ANC) out of its sanctuary in Mozambique. South African diplomats leaped at the offer, although there were many in the South African Defense Force and South African intelligence community who weren't very pleased with the decision.

Nevertheless, a non-aggression pact called the Nkomati Accord was signed on March 15, 1984, accompanied by the spectacle of a black, pro-Soviet, Marxist-Leninist dictator shaking hands with the President of white-ruled South Africa. Both Pretoria and Maputo felt it wouldn't take long for RENAMO to fold its tent and collapse.

Instead, RENAMO got stronger. It has stepped up its activities and Maputo is in a virtual state of seige. If it weren't for the sizable number of foreign troops, mostly Zimbabweans, but also the usual Soviet surrogates—1,000 East Germans, 4,000 Cubans, and 1,500 Tanzanians—the rebels would quickly overthrow the Marxist dictatorship.

But just as it seems the Marxists may come tumbling down, in rushes the United States State Department to try and prop him up. They think American aid to this bloodthirsty, anti-American Marxist thug would "wean away" Mozambique from the Soviet Union. Unfortunately, the State Department has labored for years under the crazy notion that it is possible to coax countries out of the Soviet orbit with bribes of American aid and low-cost capital loans from unprincipled American bankers.

Meanwhile, Mozambique's bleeding agony is prolonged by State Department attempts to prop up the communists. If the State Department really wanted to help Mozambique, it would direct its efforts toward a ceasefire and negotiations between RENAMO and FRELIMO. The longer the communists refuse to negotiate with RENAMO, the stronger the rebel movement becomes. They continue to stall at their peril.

In 1986 more woes were added to the Machel regime as RENAMO successfully stepped up its military action against the Marxist oligarchy.

More and more of Mozambique's countryside was coming under the control of the freedom fighters. Morale plummeted among Machel's FRELIMO forces and many fled across the border into neighboring Malawi.

Unfortunately for them, they were rounded up by the Malawi authorities and handed back to the tender mercies of their former comrades. Many of these repatriated soldiers were promptly executed by the Mozambican communists.

Matters came to a head in September 1986. Machel and his entourage of Soviet and Cuban military advisors visited northern Mozambique to assess the situation. Since RENAMO was using southern Malawi turf as staging areas for operations against FRELIMO forces in northern Mozambique, Machel's Soviet masters convinced him to pressure Malawi to eliminate the RENAMO presence therein.

Machel arranged a meeting with President Banda of Malawi. As if to underscore his point, he was accompanied by the socialist Zambian President Kenneth Kaunda and the Marxist Prime Minister of Zimbabwe Robert Mugabe to the meeting. Both Zambia and Zimbabwe depend upon Mozambique for access to the sea for their imports and exports. They had an economic stake as well in expressing ideological solidarity with Machel. This cabal pressured Banda to toss RENAMO out of Malawi. To stress the point Machel even engaged in a show of blatant saber-rattling by threatening to ring the Malawi-Mozambique border with Soviet-supplied missiles.

Caving in to this pressure, Banda told RENAMO it would have to vacate his country. Instead of meekly slinking back into Mozambique like thieves in the night, RENAMO stormed back and launched a broadside of attacks upon FRELIMO-held villages. Within a short period of time, it had captured several strategic towns in northern Mozambique.

Yes, the Soviets had given Machel some bad advice. For the first time he publicly admitted that his government had lost control of portions of Mozambique. His Soviet-suggested strategy had blown up in his face.

On October 19, 1986, the Soviet-supplied aircraft carrying Machel back to Maputo from a meeting in Zambia wandered off course and flew into a mountain just inside the South African-Mozambican border, killing the Marxist leader.

The death of Machel, however, made no difference to the goal of RENAMO—a free Mozambique. On October 28th RENAMO President Alfonso Dklakama issued an ultimatum to the communist regime that the freedom fighters were prepared to grant an amnesty to FRELIMO subject to two conditions: "1.) The withdrawal of all foreign mercenaries from Mozambique; 2.) The holding of general elections."[8]

"This is FRELIMO's last chance to avoid total military defeat. If FRELIMO rejects these reasonable conditions RENAMO has no option but to press on with the final conquest. The choice of continued war or immediate peace is on FRELIMO's doorstep. . . ."[9]

FRELIMO chose war and ignored the ultimatum; today it is pinning its hopes on being bailed out by the West, especially the United States. It is no secret that the U.S. State Department has long been pursuing its pipe dream of "weaning away" Mozambique from the Soviet empire. Since no country has ever been weaned away from the Soviets, the State Department faces a monumental task. Unfortunately, that hasn't slowed its determination in the least and it is desperately seeking methods to bail out the Marxist regime in Mozambique.

One of State's more hare-brained schemes is a $600 million "Beira Corridor" effort to rebuild the transportation and oil pipeline network between the Mozambican port of Beira and the Zimbabwean border town of Mutare. What makes this scheme so preposterous is that it runs through RENAMO-controlled territory. The freedom fighters are already attacking and destroying the current roads, pipeline and railway between Beira and Mutare. What makes any rational person believe they will not do the same to the proposed new facilities? But then one seldom expects the State Department to be realistic.

So the guerrilla war continues with the communist forces confined to the large cities where they have been systematically surrounded and cut off from the rest of the country. Soldiers in these areas dare not venture five kilometers from the center of the city and are only re-supplied by air or by heavily armed convoys risking the RENAMO gauntlet.

The winds of change are blowing in another direction. Mozambique is on the verge of becoming the first country to defect from the iron grip of the Soviet slave empire and take her place among the free nations of the world—in spite of U.S. State Department efforts to derail this process.

Thus on both coasts of Africa the desire to be free from Marxist tyranny has erupted into armed conflict. Our policymakers should pay heed to this phenomenon because it means the beginning of the end of the Brezhnev Doctrine.

1. Dahnind and Breytenbach, *UNITA* (Kwasha: UNITA Press, 1984), p. 45.

2. Ibid., p. 46.

3. Dan Sisk, "Missing Opportunity in Angola and Mozambique: The Future of Constructive Engagement," Republican Study Committee Report (October 18, 1985), p. 3.

4. "Costly Rebel Victory in a Land God Forgot," *The Washington Times* (October 9, 1985).

5. Jack Wheeler, From Rovuma to Maputo: Mozambique's Guerrilla War," *Reason* (December 1985), p. 36.

6. Ibid.

7. Interview with Secretary-General Evo Frenandes, Mozambique National Resistance, *Journal of Defense and Diplomacy* (September 1985), p. 48.

8. Message to the United States, President Alfonso Dhlakama, RENAMO, Oct. 28, 1986.

9. Ibid.

17

Purging The Mongols

"The ultimate weapon of the West," philosopher Sidney Hook said, "is not the hydrogen bomb or any other weapon, but the passion for freedom and the willingness to die for it if necessary. Once the Kremlin is convinced that we will use this weapon to prevent it from subjugating the world to its will, we will have the best assurance of peace. Once the Kremlin believes that this willingness to fight for freedom at all costs is absent, that it has been eroded by neutralist fears and pacifist wishful thinking, it will blackmail the free countries of the world into capitulation and succeed where Hitler failed."[1]

A graphic example of the consequences of the erosion of which Hook speaks is what has happened as a result of the so-called post-Vietnam attitude of the United States.

After the communists won the war in Vietnam, the United States indulged in an orgy of self-flagellation. "No more Vietnams," everyone said. While the U.S. went on a guilt trip, the Soviet Mongol Marxist-Leninist Empire went on the offensive. The Soviets invaded Afghanistan, subverted Angola, Mozambique and, well-disguised, Nicaragua. But something happened in these countries as forces of Soviet imperialism sought to impose their control. The people rose up in rebellion against their new colonial masters.

This shouldn't come as any surprise. Historically, the weak rising up to battle the strong in the arrogance of their power is nothing new. It is the human will, more than any other force or factor, that makes history, despite the denials of pop psychohistorians. The Afghans, Angolans, Mozambicans, Nicaraguans and others, tucked away in far corners of the world, don't pay attention to these soothsayers of doom.

They have taken up arms against the Soviet Empire and have committed themselves to its defeat, no matter how long it may take.

A communist regime, once in power, makes war upon the entire population under its control. It does not permit citizens to be neutral—they must be either for the regime or against it. A Marxist government clearly creates the hate and discontent that can easily feed a revolutionary movement. Brian Crozier, in his study of the rebellious personality, pointed out that "the frustrations that explode into rebellion are . . . more likely to accumulate in the single-party state, which denies them an outlet."[2]

All communist states are single-party states as a matter of doctrine and allow no opposition. When people discover how harsh communism can be, it doesn't take much imagination to figure out that the communist regime's harshness could persuade a considerable portion of the population to side with an anti-communist insurgency should one develop in their country.

Those "prophets" proclaiming the permanence of a communist regime also ignore the record of history in making their prognostications.

The word "guerrilla" originated in a country that defied the world's most massive military machine of its time. Spain, where the word was coined, was invaded by Napoleon Bonaparte, one of the world's greatest military geniuses, who had assembled one of the world's finest armies.

Spain was a poor country, her military might negligible. Her king had abandoned her and no other outstanding leaders were available to command the few men they had. In short, Spain seemed an easy target for Napoleon's military machine. But nobody convinced the Spanish people that to struggle against one such as Napoleon was an exercise in futility.

High in Spain's rugged mountains, men assembled in unmappable tiny towns. On their own authority, one after another, they formally declared war on the conqueror of Europe. Napoleon's army roared through their country like a raging storm and defeated them in battle after battle. At one point only two narrow peninsulas in all of Spain and Portugal were held by these 19th century freedom fighters. But they would not give up!

For six years, until Napoleon fell, no French soldier or official could cross any part of Spain without an escort of at least 50 men. If they foolishly tried, they never reached their destination alive. Napoleon sent one of his armies under his best marshal to attack one of the two peninsular redoubts. The army starved outside of the defense lines because the people there would rather die than give the enemy a crust of bread. Napoleon went in exile to St. Helena and Spain regained her freedom.

Today, as mentioned earlier, there are true wars of liberation being fought by the oppressed in communist dominated states. It is only a matter of time before others erupt elsewhere in the Soviets' far-flung empire. The shoe is now on the other foot. In 1967 Che Guevara gleefully proclaimed, "How close and bright would the future appear if two, three, many Vietnams, flowered on the face of the globe, with their quota of death and immense tragedies, with their daily heroism, with their repeated blows against imperialism, obliging it to dispense its forces under the lash of the world."[3]

Like lap dogs, our Jane Fondas and cowardly politicians took Guevara's cue and howled, "No more Vietnams," while the Soviet-Mongols aimed to create "two, three, many Vietnams." In the 1970s they did just that. But now Guevara's words are beginning to mock his Marxist comrades as, indeed, "two, three, many Vietnams" are breaking out against imperialism all over the world. It is Soviet imperialism that is on the receiving end.

It is this fact that exposed the mortal danger for the Soviet-Mongols. It exposes an overlooked weakness of the Soviet-Mongols's Marxist-Leninist creed of irreversibility of Marxism once it is imposed upon a society. If one of their colonies ever threw off the Soviet yoke in a war of liberation, it would explode the myth of communist invincibility and give renewed hope to others in the Soviet empire. This problem must cause many sleepless nights for Soviet masters in the Kremlin as it dawns on their restless subjects that communism is neither inevitable nor irreversible. It is for this reason that the Soviets have poured so much effort and material into Angola in their recent efforts to destroy Savimbi's UNITA guerrillas.

Soviet theoreticians and apologists can explain away an event like Grenada by saying it was an outside power that drove out the Marxist regime, not an indigenous people's movement. Therefore, in their eyes, because of this outside force, the Brezhnev doctrine still holds true. But let one liberation movement succeed in a Soviet colony and the communist myth is exposed for all to see. Already there are eight wars of liberation against communist regimes currently underway throughout the world.

When Guevara gleefully wished for "many Vietnams", he and his Marxist colleagues believed such situations would drain not only the resources of the Free World, but more important, its will to resist. Now it is the Soviets' resources that are being drained. Even though the Soviets' will to resist is apparently more determined than the West's, that too could change. As more and more of their subjects rise up against them it has got to have a detrimental effect upon their will to be constantly running around the world trying to put out brushfire wars in their far-flung colonies.

It is to be hoped that the West will gain courage from this heroic struggle and realize that the Soviet-Mongols can be defeated. As Jonas Savimbi so elegantly put it, "I think it must be the Third World that has to give the West the courage to oppose the Soviet Union and stand up its ideals, not the other way around—to provide a cure for what Solzhenitsyn calls the 'Western disease.' That is why we say 'UNITA is the key to Angola, Angola is the key to Africa. Africa is the key to the West.' "[4]

One of the most eloquent advocates of freedom, Aleksandr Solzhenitsyn, pleads with the West, and in particular the United States: "I understand that you love freedom, but in our crowded world you have to pay a tax for freedom. You cannot love freedom just for yourselves and quietly agree to a situation where the majority of humanity over the greater part of the globe is being subjected to violence and oppression.

"The Communist ideology is to destroy your society. This

has been their aim for 125 years and has never changed. Only the methods have changed a little. When there is detente, peaceful co-existence, and trade, they will still insist the ideological war must continue! And what is ideological war? It is a focus of hatred, this continued repetition of the oath to destroy the Western world.

"But a concentration of world evil, of hatred for humanity is taking place and it is fully determined to destroy your society. Must you wait until it comes with a crowbar to break through your borders, until the young men of America have to fall defending the border of their continent?"[5]

The young men of America don't have to fall because there are millions of others throughout the world who are willing to do the fighting—the freedom fighters waging wars of liberation against the Soviet-Mongols. They don't ask for our sons and brothers to fight shoulder to shoulder with them; they ask for help of other kinds: material and moral support.

In the 1940s the United States proudly proclaimed itself to be the arsenal of democracy. Then, we committed not only our blood but made our tremendous industrial capacity available to defeat at the same time the warlords of Japan and the evil socialism of Adolph Hitler. Today, even though the menace is greater than four decades ago, we can help the cause of freedom by furnishing arms and money to those who ask.

Testifying before Congress on aid to the Angolan freedom fighters, Rep. Jack Kemp (R-N.Y.) said, "The U.S. stands on the side of freedom, self-determination and human rights, in sharp contrast to the human misery, suffering, starvation, and dying economies that Soviet imperialism has brought to the African continent. We should make it clear to the rest of the world that the threat posed by the Soviets and Cubans will be met, and that the U.S. intends to support those people in Angola who share our commitment to democratic government and open political societies."[6]

Congressman Kemp specifically mentioned Angola, but his comments are equally applicable throughout the world where people are struggling to cast off the murderous yoke of Soviet-imposed tyranny.

Our task is clear: we in the West, especially the United States, the land of the free, should pursue a policy of helping slaves become free. "The policy best suited to the world in which we find ourselves today is one of generous military and economic aid to anti-communist insurgencies, but without controls," Rep. Kemp said. "It is our moral obligation—and very much in our national interest—to give those who are fighting our battles elsewhere out of our abundance the tools they need to do the job, and we should not seek to control the way in which those tools are used. The freedom fighters may sometimes make obviously incorrect use of what we give them; we may sometimes disagree with their strategy and tactics; but their lives and homes are at risk; ours are not. They are caught up in the grimmest of human tragedies, and in general their judgment is at least as good as ours. So long as the material resources we provide are used for the purposes for which they were given, and with reasonable efficiency, we have no complaint.

"This, then, should be the cornerstone of our policy towards freedom fighters throughout the world: we must decide on principle that we shall assist insurgencies against communist regimes wherever they may appear. . . ."[7]

In addition, aid and diplomatic recognition must be withheld from pro-Soviet regimes, letting the Soviets, with their almost non-existent domestic economy, bail out their colonial proxies. We shouldn't allow our "Venetian-type" banks to cut deals advantageous to the Soviet-Mongol empire. If socialism is such a wonderful system, by all means, let's give them the opportunity to prove it.

As Chief Buthelezi said, "It is a historical truism that every oppressed people have the responsibility of liberating themselves."[8] The oppressed people of the world are fighting back and they look to the United States for help and inspiration. All we have to do is give them the tools and they will take on the task of dismantling the evil edifices throughout the world created by the ideology of Marxist-Leninist communism—the enemy of all men and women on this planet. Theirs will be the glorious task of consigning this evil to the dustbin of history.

1. Sidney Hook, *Political Power and Personal Freedom* (New York: Criterion Books, 1959), p. 426.

2. Brian Crozier, *The Rebel* (Boston: Beacon Press, 1960), p. 68.

3. George Lavan, ed., *Guevera Speaks* (New York: Pathfinder Press, 1980), p. 159.

4. "Angola's Anti-Soviet Guerrillas," *Reason* (April 1984), p. 27.

5. Address by Aleksandr Solzhenitsyn to AFL-CIO in New York on July 9, 1975.

6. "Aid to Freedom Fighters: Action, Inaction, Counteraction," *The Freedom Fighter*, Freedom League, Wash., D.C. (November 1985), p. 5.

7. Charles Moser, *Combat on Communist Territory* (Wash., D.C.: Free Congress Foundation, 1985), p. 213.

8. Statement of M.G. Buthelezi, Chief Minister, Kwazulu, in Ulandi on March 9, 1984.

Appendix A

The Alvor Agreement

(Note: The Portuguese State and the national liberation movements of Angola, FNLA, MPLA, and UNITA, met in Alvor, Algarve, from January 10-15, 1975, in order to discuss the independence of Angola. They agreed on the following which was subsequently disregarded and breached by the MPLA and the Soviets.)

Chapter 1
Angola's Independence

Article 1
The Portuguese State acknowledges that the liberation movements FNLA, MPLA and UNITA are the sole representatives of the Angolan people.

Article 2
The Portuguese State solemnly acknowledges the right of the Angolan people to independence.

Article 3
Within its present geographical and political limits, Angola constitutes one indivisible unity. In this context, Cabinda is an integral and inalienable part of the Angolan territory.

Article 4
Full independence and sovereignty of Angola shall be solemnly proclaimed on the 11th of November 1975.

Article 5
Until the proclamation of independence, political power rests with the High Commissioner and the Transitional Govern-

ment to come into the power on the 31st of January 1975.

Article 6
The Portuguese State and the three liberation movements formalize, on the date of the signing of the present agreements, the general cease-fire which is already being observed by the respective armed forces within the whole territory of Angola. From that date onwards, all acts of violence not ordered by the authorities with the view to avoiding internal disorder or external aggression, shall be considered illegal.

Article 7
After the cease-fire, the armed forces of FNLA, MPLA and UNITA shall settle in their rightful regions and localities until the execution of the special provisions set in Chapter IV of the present agreement.

Article 8
Until the end of the transition period, the Portuguese State pledges to progressively transfer to the Angolan organs of sovereignty all the powers it holds and exercises in Angola.

Article 9
Upon conclusion of the present agreements, all patriotic actions undertaken in the course of the struggle for the liberation of Angola which would have been considered punishable by the law in force at the time when they took place, are considered totally pardoned.

Article 10
The independent state of Angola shall exercise its sovereignty totally and freely, internally as well as externally. . . .

Chapter III
Transitional Government

Article 14
The Transitional Government is presided over and led by the Presidential College.

Article 15
The Presidential College is constituted by three members, one from each liberation movement and has, as its main duty, the

direction and coordination of the Transitional Government.

Article 16
The Presidential College can, as long as it deems fit, consult the High Commissioner on affairs related to the activities of the Government.

Article 17
The deliberations of the Transitional Government are adopted by a majority of two thirds under the rotating presidency of the members of the Presidential College.

Article 18
The Transitional Government is constituted of the following ministries: Interior, Information, Labour and Social Security, Economy, Planning and Finance, Justice, Transport and Communications, Health and Social Affairs, Public Works, Housing and Urbanization, Education and Culture, Agriculture and Natural Resources.

Article 19
The following state secretaries are henceforth created.
  (a) Two secretariats in the Ministry of the Interior.
  (b) Two state secretariats in the Ministry of Information.
  (c) Two secretariats in the Ministry of Labour and Social Security.
  (d) Three state secretariats in the Ministry of Economy, with the following respective designations: Secretariat for Commerce and Tourism, Secretariat for Industry and Energy and Secretariat for Fisheries.

Article 20
The ministers of the Transitional Government are appointed in equal proportion from the FNLA, the MPLA and UNITA by the President of the Portuguese Republic.

Article 21
Considering the transitional character of the Government, the distribution of ministries is to be done according to the following:
  (a) The President of the Portuguese Republic shall designate the Ministers of Economy, Public Works, Hous-

ing and Urbanization, and Transport and Communications;
  (b) The FNLA shall appoint the Ministers of the Interior, Health and Social Affairs, and Agriculture;
  (c) MPLA shall appoint the Ministers of Information, Finance and Justice;
  (d) UNITA shall appoint the Ministers of Education, Work and Social Security, Culture and Natural Resources.

Article 22
The state secretariats foreseen in the present agreements are distributed as follows:
  (a) The FNLA shall designate one Secretary of State for Information, one Secretary of State for Labour and Social Security and the Secretary of State for Commerce and Tourism;
  (b) The MPLA shall designate one Secretary of State for the Interior, one Secretary of State for Labour and Social Security, and the Secretary of State for Industry and Energy;
  (c) UNITA shall designate one Secretary of State for the Interior, one Secretary of State for Information and the Secretary of State for Fisheries.

Article 23
The Transitional Government can create new posts for secretaries and under secretaries of state as long as it respects the rule of political heterogeneity in their distribution.

Article 24
Duties of the Transitional Government:
  (a) Oversee and cooperate in the leading of the decolonizing process until total independence.
  (b) Supervise the whole public administration; ensure its normal functioning and promote the accession of Angolan citizens to responsible positions.
  (c) Conduct the internal policy.
  (d) Prepare and ensure the holding of general elections for the Angolan constituent assembly.
  (e) Exercise by decree the legislative function and elabo-

rate decrees, regulations and instructions for the
orderly fulfillment of the laws.
(f) Guarantee the security of persons and property in
cooperation with the High Commissioner.
(g) Reorganize the Angolan judiciary.
(h) Define the economic, financial and monetary policy
and create the necessary framework for the rapid
development of the Angolan economy.
(i) Guarantee and safeguard all collective and individual
rights and liberties.

Article 25
The Presidential College and all ministers are collectively
responsible for the activities of the Government.

Article 26
The Transitional Government shall not be dismissed on the
initiative of the High Commissioner. Should any need for the
alteration of its constitution arise, it shall be effected by
agreement between the High Commissioner and the liberation movements.

Article 27
The High Commissioner and the Presidential College shall
look for ways and means of solving all the difficulties
resulting from government activities within the spirit of
friendship and by reciprocal consultation. . . .

Chapter VI
General Elections for the Angolan Constituent Assembly

Article 40
The Transitional Government shall organize general elections for a constituent assembly within nine months from the
31st of January 1975, the date of its coming into power.

Article 41
The candidates for the Constituent Assembly shall be pre-
sented by the liberation movements only, i.e., the FNLA, the
MPLA and UNITA, the only true representatives of the
Angolan people.

Article 42

After the installation of the Transitional Government, a Central Commission constituted in equal parts by members from each liberation movement shall elaborate the bill of rights and prepare the elections for the Constituent Assembly.

Article 43

After the bill of rights has been approved by the Transitional Government and upon its promulgation by the Presidential College, the Central Commission shall:

   (a) Lay down a law for elections;
   (b) Organize the voters' register;
   (c) Register the list of candidates for the election of the Constituent Assembly presented by the liberation movements.

Article 44

The bill of rights in force until the Angolan Constitution takes effect shall not contradict the terms of the present agreements.

Chapter VII
Angolan Nationality

Article 45

The Portuguese State and the three liberation movements, the FNLA, the MPLA, and UNITA, pledge to act in concert in order to eliminate all sequels of colonialism. To this end, the FNLA, the MPLA and UNITA reaffirm their policy of non-discrimination according to which Angolan citizenship is defined by birth or by domicile provided that the people domiciled in Angola identify themselves with the aspirations of the Angolan nation through a conscious option.

Article 46

The FNLA, the MPLA and UNITA henceforth undertake the compromise and consider as Angolan citizens all individuals born in Angola, unless they declare that they desire to maintain their present nationality or opt for another; the terms and time limits will be defined later.

Article 47
Individuals not born in Angola but settled in that country are guaranteed the faculty to apply for Angolan citizenship in accordance with the rules established in the fundamental law.

Article 48
Special agreements to be studied at the level of the mixed parity commission shall determine the conditions of granting Angolan citizenship to Portuguese citizens residing in Angola and Angolan citizens residing in Portugal. . . .

Chapter XI
General Provisions

Article 58
Any issues arising from the application of the present agreements which cannot be solved within the terms of Article 27 shall be resolved through negotiation between the Portuguese Government and the liberation movements.

Article 59
The Portuguese State, the FNLA, the MPLA and UNITA, faithful to the socio-political conceptions repeatedly affirmed by their leaders, reaffirm their respect for the principles consecrated in the Charter of the United Nations and in the Universal Declaration of Human Rights, as well as their active repudiation of all forms of racial discrimination, namely "Apartheid."

Article 60
The present agreement shall come into force immediately after the sanction by the President of the Portuguese Republic. The declaration of the Portuguese Government, the FNLA, the MPLA and UNITA stresses the climate of perfect cooperation and cordiality in which the negotiations took place and congratulate themselves on the conclusion of the present agreements which satisfy the just aspirations of the Angolan people and enhance the pride of the Portuguese people, from now on bound by profound ties of friendship and the objective of constructive cooperation for the well-being of

Angola, Portugal, Africa and the world.

Signed in Alvor, Algarve, on the 15th of January 1975, in fourfold in the Portuguese language.

Appendix B
RENAMO's Manifesto

1. The Mozambican National Resistance is an organization dedicated to the establishment and defense of democracy in Mozambique and to the well-being of all the Mozambican People without distinction of race, tribe, colour, religion or place of origin.
2. The Mozambican National Resistance is dedicated to the eradication of all anti-democratic tendencies which threaten democracy in Mozambique, particularly communism, fascism, racialism, tribalism, and religious discrimination.
3. The Mozambican National Resistance is dedicated to the establishment of constitutional rule in Mozambique based on a democratic constitution with specific guarantees for the human rights, life, property and human dignity of all Mozambicans, of all persons of Mozambican nationality and of all residents of Mozambique.
4. The Mozambican National Resistance is dedicated to the establishment of a national constitution guaranteeing the formation of a government based on periodic and free general elections, with the election interval fixed by the constitution.
5. The Mozambican National Resistance is dedicated to the establishment of a national constitution guaranteeing the political rights of every Mozambican and the right of every adult Mozambican to form or participate in any political organization of his choice; to propose himself or others for election to public office; and to elect or be elected to such office.
6. The Mozambican National Resistance is dedicated to the

establishment of a national constitution with separation of the executive, legislative and judicial powers, and with a Supreme Court which will be the supreme authority on constitutional questions.

7. The Mozambican National Resistance is dedicated to the establishment of a national constitution guaranteeing religious freedom and the right of every person to practice his religion fully and without fear.

8. The Mozambican National Resistance is dedicated to the establishment of a national constitution guaranteeing freedon of speech, freedom of the press, freedom of association and freedom of movement.

9. The Mozambican National Resistance is dedicated to the establishment of a national constitution guaranteeing the right of every person to acquire, hold and dispose of property, and guaranteeing, moreover, that no person may be deprived of his property excepting in circumstances approved by the constitution and through due process of law.

10. The Mozambican National Resistance, recognizing existing regional and ethnic realities and aspiration, and wishing to guarantee the rights of all sections of the Mozambican People, is dedicated to the establishment of a national constitution creating a federal system of government which will allow each of the country's provinces to exercise authority over matters of mainly local or provincial importance. The powers of provincial governments will have their own constitutions which may not in any case conflict with the National Constitution.

Appendix C
Regeneration of Mozambique

The Mozambican National Resistance has as its principal tasks:

1. To liberate the Mozambican People from the oppressive communist rule of the Machel regime through: intensifying the armed struggle and increasing military, political, economic and other pressures against the Machelists throughout Mozambique until their inevitable collapse.

2. To establish a provisional government to administer the country for a period not exceeding two years after the removal of the Machel regime. The provisional government will have as its principal tasks:

   a. to insure the dissolution of all communist political, administrative, economic, social and other structures in Mozambique.

   b. to draft a democratic national constitution for Mozambique, based on the equal rights and duties of all Mozambicans and the equality before the law of all Mozambicans.

   c. to convene a constituent assembly composed of the duly elected representatives of the Mozambican People throughout the country to study and, if necessary, amend the draft constitution and to approve it.

   d. to organize and hold free elections throughout Mozambique for representatives who will then form the new democratic Government of Mozambique.

Index